The Charles Schwab
Stock Rip-Off

Dr. La Crone is available as an expert witness and as a consultant for shareholders' litigation. He may be reached at lacrone@gmail.com

Visit www.booksurge.com to order additional copies.

The Charles Schwab Stock Rip-Off

How Management Insiders Are Looting Stock Investors' Money

Michael La Crone, MBA, DBA

2009

The Charles Schwab
Stock Rip-Off

To Chandra Wati—whose love, loyalty, and devotion sustain my happiness. To my mother, father, brother, and nephew Woody—all whose lives were cut short by the use of tobacco. Thanks go to my niece Tess La Crone Love, CPA, Paul Weisser, PhD, Ferdinand Pecora, and Tom L. (Burlingame); the libraries of Alameda County, San Lorenzo, San Bruno, and Burlingame; Pat McKelvey, Christian Flores, and Gail Cato, BookSurge Editor, for their valuable advice and editorial assistance, and the critical comments from Professor Jesse Dillard, and Michael Lapuz, all have added value to my life and work.

INTRODUCTION

Fraud: Some willful act or device calculated to influence or mislead a person to his prejudice. (Elements of Business Law: Ernest W. Huffcut 1905)

Embezzlement: The fraudulent appropriation of property by one lawfully entrusted with its possession. (Black's Law Dictionary 6th ed. West Publishing Co. 1990)

Illusory Promise: A promise in which the promisor does not bind himself to do anything and hence it furnishes no basis for a contract because of the lack of consideration. (Black's Law Dictionary 6th ed. West Publishing Co. 1990)

Self-Serving: Self-serving implies that a person is in a position of power. That power provides opportunities for a person to improve their personal wealth through the use of that power.

Self-dealing implies that a person is in a position of power. That person uses their power to transfer unearned wealth into their own account from the earned wealth of others.

Dr. Michael La Crone

There is a war devastating America today. This is not a war of guns and bombs, but of stealth financial manipulations using embedded information and formulas that transfer stock investors' wealth to management insiders' accounts at light speed. Their transactions are so efficient and effective they make a computerized milking machine look like covered wagon technology. This is a war of parasitic theft against an unsuspecting public. The weapons in this war are stealth, self-dealing, device, and deception. This is a war waged not only with pen, paper, and computer, but also with asymmetric information, political bribery, corrupted regulators, lies, and manipulation. This is a war of Wall Street insiders against Main Street outsiders. I have a data set that shows where twenty-five executives received over 102 million gift shares, not including optioned shares, Multiply 102 million gift shares by fifty dollars a share, and you get a sense of what this war is about. This data set is just a small sample of a few executives over a short period of time. That is the kind of killing taking place in this war. Americans must organize a counter movement that will bring justice to the victims and reparations from the offenders or they can expect more of the same.

This book is about insider traders committing fraud on stock market investors. The book is not about dilution of earnings or dilution of shareholders' value; it is about selective use of deception and device for skimming money from at-the-money (explained later) investors. The book is not about risk and reward; it is about wealth transfers from shareholders to managers. The book is not about a value-for-value exchange; it is about you lose—they win in a zero-sum transaction.

Don't let anyone tell you that this book is inclined to overstatement; on the contrary, corruption and deception in the stock market is much worse than what is articulated in this book. If the next president covers up the crimes of Wall Street (east and west), and the self-dealings of Wall Street's President Bush and his administration's connection to the stock market's corruption; it will be tantamount to willful neglect of duty and a violation of public trust. Since this was first written, Obama has been elected president, and he has done nothing to get justice for Mom and Pop investors who lost their retirement savings to stock market insiders.

Next to representative democracy, the corporation has proved to be one of the greatest inventions ever created for helping solve the economic problems of humanity. On the other hand, corporate managements and a lobbied Congress have proved a destructive force of the corporate form that can completely corrupt such an organization. The consequences of a corporation's corruption can have a devastating and blighting effects on the lives of all those who have even a remote connection to its influence.

These few pages present the argument that investors were swindled in the 2000–2001 stock market bubble. The conditions that helped to perpetuate this theft have not been altered and continue today in 2009 as they did in 2001. The people who carried out this monumental rip-off are still taking investors' money. In 2000–2001, investors were lured into buying ownership shares in corporations on the pretext of a risk/return ownership position in the profit or loss of a corporate investment. What they received was a transfer of their wealth to corporate managers through deception and the use of the manipulative device of stock gifts and options.

Recently, the Wall Street-controlled Securities and Exchange Commission has changed the rules to liberalize insider looting of shareholder money by allowing corporate boards to give themselves and corporate managers' gift shares and awards of shares. This is tantamount to counterfeiting money. Management insiders are dumping truckloads of free and optioned shares on unsuspecting stock market investors.

- As long as it is a prearranged plan, the Securities and Exchange Commission (SEC) Rule 10b5-1 allows insiders to set up a program for trading a company's stock even if, as insiders, they come into material nonpublic information. These management insiders are trading for their own account on shareholders' wealth.

- Financial computer simulations can predict with a fair amount of accuracy what a company's stock price will be on a certain date. This is especially true in cyclical industries.

- Not only can directors give themselves and managers stock options, they can surrender a portion of their options back to the company to cover taxes and the strike price costs for the options. Essentially making the options not only risk free, but also a free money gifts of shareholders' investment funds.

This is embezzlement of shareholders' money, but when the law says it's legal, shareholders can do little against being legally robbed. The current corporate management abuses of trust and fiduciary responsibility are a financial crime against mom-and-pop investors as well as against public pension funds. Because stock equity wealth transfers are legal does not diminish their criminality. Slavery was legal, and it was criminal. Hitler's treatment of the Jews was legal, and it was criminal. The looting of investors' pension money is legal, and it too is criminal.

Like a diagnosis that explains how and why a patient is made ill by intestinal parasites, this book explains how and why retirement funds of many investors were bankrupted by parasitic financial manipulations1 of the stock market with stock options. Some concepts in this commentary may seem, at times, obscure for those who have not studied options, but unavoidably, explaining the process of how and why investors were ripped off is a process of uncovering the obscure. I have provided endnotes to overcome such difficulties. On behalf of "investors" who lost their money to management insiders from the stocks of companies like Qualcomm, Broadcom, Ciena, Conexant Systems, JDS Uniphase, Sycamore Networks, Terayon, Global Crossing, the same analysis and conclusions apply to at least a hundred others. Many of these companies have in common the sales efforts of George Gilder who, as a self-appointed technology expert and confessed liar, acted as their shill. These firms were not fly-by-night dot-com start-ups, but billion-dollar capitalized companies.

Had investors received adequate information and had they been aware that their money would be transferred to management through gifts and options, this discussion would not be about parasitic financial practices by Wall Street bankers, stock brokers, and corporate management, but instead, about Santa Claus investments. Only Santa Claus could afford these types of equity wealth transfer gifts. The enormity of these wealth giveaways would further suggest that if Santa Claus had lost as much in retirement savings as Mom and Pop, he would be fuming. Management insiders taking free and optioned shares to cash out unsuspecting stock market investors is equivalent to a parasitic financial infection.

Essentially, Wall Street bankers, stock brokers, and corporate management insiders are free loading on gift and optioned stock funded by the paid-in capital that took outside investors

30, 40, 50,or more years to save for their retirements. If you think this is okay and looting grandpa's and grandma's pension funds are just a part of the free market, then it will be okay for your pension funds to be looted. Former President Bush (number 2) and his appointee Treasury Secretary Henry (Goldman Sachs) Paulson are constantly referring to the importance of the free market. What they really mean is that they and their friends are free to self-deal in the public's money by looting the free market. Looting investor's retirement money is not a part of the free market. As will be explained, the stock market today is a piggy bank for insiders. Wall Street insiders like Mr. Paulson have turned our economic democracy into slavery economics.

This book is a patchwork of information on current conditions and forces driving the stock market. The arguments are valid, honest, and consistent, but not always in linear form and are at times repetitive perforce a lack of editorial input. For those who have a compulsion to edit, read the book for ideas, after you finish editing, send me a copy of your critique so that I may incorporate your work into my next edition.

Of course, I expect to be criticized for writing such an inflammatory book, but nothing could be more inflammatory or villainous than stealing retirement savings from Mom and Pop and widows and orphans for the cause of vanity.

As you will read in the following pages, Mr. Schwab is a poster boy for sleazy parasitic self-dealing. If you want to save your retirement—don't talk to Chuck. As a trusted gatekeeper, Mr. Schwab is in a position to know whose money is in what accounts, how much, and when to cash out for maximum transfer of investor money for his own account. Like so much wastepaper, Schwab just "swept" more than four hundred million dollars of investors' funds into his account. Some readers will say that I am vilifying Mr. Schwab, but he has done all the work himself. I am merely reporting the facts. Mr. Schwab and other CEOs who are pocketing free money at investors' expense are indulging in a deceitful one-sided enrichment through unconscionable self-dealing. Their behavior demands justice, political, court, or street.

Essentially, Mr. Schwab is selling investors an embedded obligation to let him pay himself out of their equity funds. Between 2004 and 2006, Mr. Schwab sold over 4 million shares of "gift stock" given to him by the Board of Directors (MarketWatch.com 10-26-2006), thereby cashing out investors' ownership money. Simply, these are investors who sacrificed for hour-by-hour savings given over to larcenist by way of deception. Divide 4 million by 100= 40,000. This means that 40,000 new investors who bought 100 shares were cashed out by Mr. Schwab. You have heard of an LBO (Leveraged Buy Out), this is a LCO (Leveraged Cash Out). Assuming no other transactions, it would take 40,000 new investors to pay the same price as the first 40,000 for the first investors to get their money out at the same price. Mr. Schwab will not expose his free money gains to loss by buying his company's stock. He can get all the free stock he wants. He expects new investors to cover this pillage. Every dollar of investors' earned money taken by Mr. Schwab is unearned personal gain. In any language this is looting of investors' money by Schwab, and it is just one symptom associated with the systemically perverse activity of equity takings by thousands of corporate insiders.

BETRAYED TRUST

Why is there such a huge disparity between Main Street investors' massive stock value losses and the hundreds of millions of dollars in Wall Street insiders' gains? You would think that if Wall Street were working for Main Street there would be mutually beneficial gains or mutually detrimental losses. Why can't the stock investing baker and the barber connect the dots between their losses and Wall Street's gains? My take is that the whole stock investment process is too abstract for the average person to understand. The pension investor has to rely on trust in those who make the investment decisions to be trustworthy and honest fiduciaries. The problem is that insiders like Mr. Schwab (a fiduciary) see these investors as dumb money. That is how Mr. Schwab describes those who lost their money in the stock market in 2002. The same logic drives the management's financial decisions at Goldman Sachs, JP Morgan Chase, Merrill Lynch, Citigroup, Morgan Stanley, Lehman Brothers, Bear Stearns, Microsoft, Oracle, American Express, and Occidental Petroleum to name just a few. A form of financial parasitism is going on in the stock market that is difficult to understand, and those in charge who have a fiduciary duty to protect and inform are the parasites.

Main Street mom-and-pop stock investors do not have a clue about how management insiders are using their 401 (K) stock investment money as a slush fund for their personal gain. Mom and Pop do not understand the enormous amount of financial manipulation in place to transfer pension fund money to insiders' personal accounts. Why? Because none of those on the take will tell. If you tell the average person that Congress, the president, and the regulatory agencies are involved in a conspiracy of silence for the benefit of Wall Street and corporate managers, you'll be looked at askance. People don't want to believe that their government's leaders have sold them out for personal gain, but as has happened to working people throughout history, it is what is happening in America today.

GRAPHS OF STOCK MARKET REALITY

The three graphs on the next page present a visual picture of the stock market. First is a graph of a company's stock price. Investors are lured into buying a company's stock because the company has a positive earnings report or a fund manager has touted its future growth possibilities. What the investor doesn't know is that management insiders are getting free shares through awards of stock, gift stock, stock options, or some other stealth form of stock equity compensation that skims the top off investors' stock investment value. If you buy a stock at $100, and it drops one cent, you lost a cent. Look at the top of the curve. It has an arrow pointing to at-the-money investors. Gift stock and stock options do not distress stock investors equally, those who bought IPO shares cheap are not touched by this skim. Only new-to-the-market investors who are at-the-money get ripped off. The skimming activity does not affect deep-in-the-money shareholders. In other words, gift stock, award of stock, and stock options are selectively adverse to at-the-money new investors. If a management insider, like Mr. Schwab, gets 1,666,000 gift shares as he did recently, you and 1,666,000 mom-and-pop shareholders will be skimmed of your stock investment value each time Mr. Schwab sells a share (between 1,000 and 10,000 a day). He knows this and now so do you. It's like owning a business, and at the end of a business day, having the manager take some of the day's sales cash, only this is your retirement savings or college fund.

GRAPH 1

Supporting Graphs
Michael R La Crone MBA, DBA

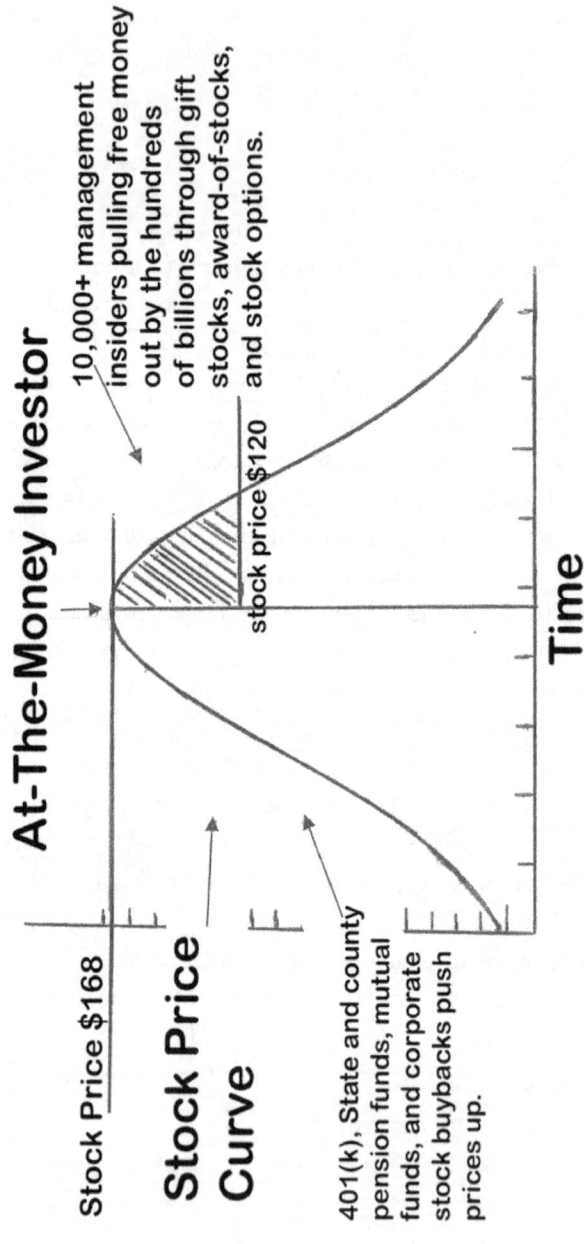

At-The-Money Investor

10,000+ management insiders pulling free money out by the hundreds of billions through gift stocks, award-of-stocks, and stock options.

stock price $120

Stock Price $168

Stock Price Curve

401(k), State and county pension funds, mutual funds, and corporate stock buybacks push prices up.

Time

The next graph shows how the deception has been justified. I cover these ideas later in the book, but it is good to introduce them with graphs. The legal justification for allowing insider self-dealing of shareholder money says that stock compensation helps managers align their interest with shareholders. This is a blatant lie, and the graph shows why. The theory does not match the reality. Actually, shareholders are in an option writer's position and managers are in a buyer's position. There is a mirror divergent zero-sum situation where shareholders lose what managers gain. Managers do not align their interests with shareholders; they compete with shareholders' money for shareholders' money. Not only is there an inverse relationship resulting in no alignment between shareholder and management, there is no valuable consideration traded in a value-for-value exchange. The curves describe a zero-sum game where management insiders have a riskless, costless, one-sided, absolute, and certain gain, and shareholders bear the total cost of an absolute and certain loss. No rational shareholder would knowingly expose his or her investment savings to such a deception.

Gain/Loss for Call Buyer (solid line) and Call Writer (dotted line)

Graph 2

Stock Option Curves

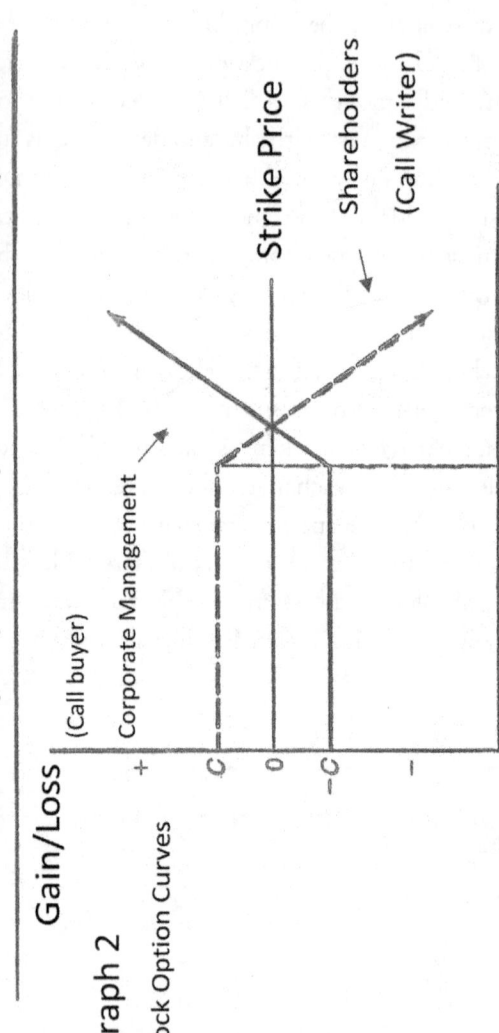

Corporate board writes self-dealing call options paid for by shareholders equity. An inverse relationship between corporate management gain and shareholders' losses. No alignment of interest. Corporate management competes with shareholders for shareholders' money.

In the back of my mind, I can hear insiders like Chuck Schwab and Henry Paulson saying to themselves: We have transferred hundreds of millions of investors' dollars into our own personal accounts, and in doing so, we have impoverished many people who do not have a clue about what happened to their money. Now it's time to put them back to work by lending them their money back to them. If some of them sense they have been defrauded and complain, we will say that they are just trying to find a scapegoat who they can blame for their own failures. The victims have successfully been given the blame for our rip-off. Our deceptions have succeeded! We have by way of deception, effectively used and betrayed the trust of investors to scam them out of their retirement savings. They earned it, and we have given their money to our children, and the children of their children.

The last graph shows what happened to mom-and-pop investors' money between 1999 and 2001 when Mr. Schwab and his managers skimmed a total of $951 million through insider self-dealing stock options. Schwab stock dropped almost a billion dollars and at-the-money investors lost 75 percent of their shareholdings. Mark Gimein reported this in Fortune, September 2, 2002, "You Bought They Sold: The Greedy Bunch." The SEC justifies this fraud by requiring a disclosure, but disclosures hide the wealth transfer in deceitfulness and omissions.

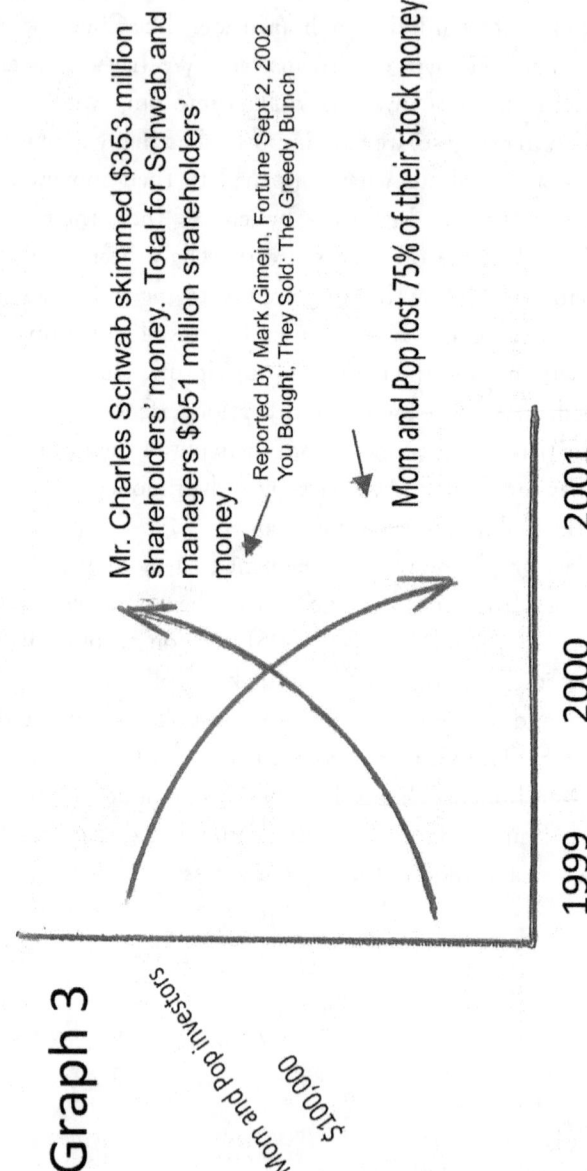

Graph 3

Mom and pop investors

$100,000

1999   2000   2001

Mr. Charles Schwab skimmed $353 million shareholders' money. Total for Schwab and managers $951 million shareholders' money.

Reported by Mark Gimein, Fortune Sept 2, 2002
You Bought, They Sold: The Greedy Bunch

Mom and Pop lost 75% of their stock money.

8

Expanding on the information contained in graph #1, is the point indicated by an investor being at-the-money. The arrow pointing to at-the-money investors represents a deep and wide pool of investors' wealth in the form of stock ownership. This wealth represents savings that may have taken thirty, forty or more years to earn.

Wealth has been transferred to a management insider who has not earned a cent of it. As a transfer of wealth, this self-dealing enrichment came to exist by the power of insiders' influence over the legitimization of a manipulative financial device justified with a lie.

A Summary of Analysis of Stock Option Compensation from the Shareholder's Point of View:

The stock market of 2000–2001 was a rip-off where many mom-and-pop investors lost much if not most of their retirement savings to an insider swindle. I use the word swindle very carefully.

After the drop in stock prices in March 2001, I could not believe that the market could wipe out so many "investors" as quickly as it did. Beyond getting caught in a seller's market, there had to be an underlying reason for the stock market to lose so much permanent value.

I began to look for who got the money, and found an article in Fortune (Sept. 2, 2002) titled "You Bought, They Sold." The article contained a list of insiders the author called the "Greedy Bunch." Charles Schwab was on the list, as was Gary Winnick of Global Crossing, Jozef Straus of JDS Uniphase, Scott Kriens of Juniper Networks, Craig McCaw of Nextel Communications,

Henry Samueli and Henry Nicholas of Broadcom, and several other insiders in whose stock many investors lost money. Come to find out, managers were manipulating option dates and revenue numbers to max out their option skim. Of course, no government regulator is willing to help defrauded shareholders get their money back plus interest they lost. These managers' great-grandchildren will be spending money thousands of investors earned.

I came to find out that these insiders used gift and optioned stock to transfer mom-and-pop shareholders' wealth to themselves by the tens of billions of dollars. Warren Buffett, commenting on the billions of dollars taken out of investors' pockets in 2000–2001 by corporate managers, said that stock market losses were "the biggest peacetime wealth transfer in history."† Transfer in the sense of wealth redistribution from shareholders to management insiders.

†Quoted in Robert F. Felton and Mark Watson, "Change Across the Board: Investors Are Angry—Directors Can Run But They Can't Hide," McKinsey Quarterly, autumn 2002, p. 7.

After reading several books and articles, I realized that this stock market rip-off was accomplished by use of a manipulative device (equity gifts and options), a justification based on lies, and deception (materially flawed disclosures). The question became, how could such a swindle be legal? After a lot of research, I wrote this book. I summarized the book into a paper titled "Four Arguments for Why Corporate Compensation in the Form of Equity Stock Options are a Fraud on the Market," and finally summarized it further into four paragraphs. There are probably many other arguments that weigh against equity options, but the four outlined below will, I am sure, convince an impartial reader that shareholders were swindled.

Summary of the arguments from the paper "Four Arguments for Why Corporate Compensation in the Form of Equity Stock Options are a Fraud on the Market":

1. Factors: (Self-dealing; commingling of managers' with shareholders' ownership interest; conflicts of interest) Insiders were allowed to use inside information for taking arbitrage gains at the expense of outside at-the-money shareholders. This was insider trading and a self-dealing conflict of interest. Unknown to investors is the fact that corporate directors are allowed to give shareholders' money to themselves, managers, corporate lawyers, and any other titled employee they deem worthy of equity options and gift shares. Section 10b5-1 allows for insider self-dealing. For example, directors can vote themselves millions of gift shares. The recipients can then give back some of the shares to pay for the taxes on the shares. Free money for insiders from shareholders' accounts!

2. Factors: (Skimming at-the-money equity interest; manipulative device) Gift and optioned stock is used as a skimming device against new at-the-money stock buyers. It does not affect most of the in-the-money shareholders, and does not affect deep-in-the-money shareholders. In other words, it is selectively adverse to new investors. See Graph #1

3. Factors: (Illusory promise; no alignment of interest; no valuable consideration for at-the-money investors) Equity stock gifts and options not only lack valuable consideration for a value-for-value exchange, but are inversely related to shareholders' inter-

est. This results in an illusory promise. That is, an empty promise contains no valid exchange value. This is a very important point because equity options create a competitive relationship between management and shareholders for shareholders' money. The justification for an equity option is that it aligns the interest of shareholders with managers, but managers receive a zero-sum risk-free gain at shareholders' expense.

There is an infinite divergence of interests between a call buyer and a call writer. See Graph #2

4. Factors: (Material misrepresentation in disclosures; zero-sum self-dealing wealth transfers) Disclosures were deceptive because they hid the real wealth transfer cost of equity gift and options to at-the-money investors who are new-to-the-market. The use of equity options is a parasitic wealth transfer dressed in the deceitful pretext of earned compensation that no informed investor with adequate knowledge would consider as an investment. This is a material manipulation of information. Regulation by information cannot and has never prevented insiders from misleading investors. Section 10 (b) of the Securities Exchange Act of 1934 is a sham regulation that provides no real protection for investors. Graph #3 applies equally well to all of the Greedy Bunch.

Conclusion: Equity stock options neither align the interest of management with shareholders nor are they an earned form of compensation. Management insiders are skimming both the retirement equity ownership and stock price appreciation of shareholders as wealth transfers.

STOCK BUYBACKS

Another important element that establishes the stock market as a pump-and-dump scheme involves stock buybacks. A primary activity of companies is to use their retained earnings for investing in research and development projects that grow their future cash flows. They also use retained earnings to pay shareholders dividends. Companies repurchase their shares as a substitute for dividends. One rationale for the repurchases is that it is a more tax-efficient way to return cash to shareholders. Management engages in repurchases if they decide that the market has undervalued its stock. Of course, this is a circular argument when management is skimming shareholders' money thereby reducing investor funds available to buy the company's shares. Another important reason to repurchase shares has to do with directors and executives' compensation. Corporate directors buy back shares to issue them to themselves and executives in exchange for their stock options. These managers are usually giving options to themselves as a performance bonus, so they have to show investors growth in earnings per share (EPS). A problem with stock options is that when too many options have been exercised, the growth of shares outstanding affects their EPS and their P/E rations.

This illustration appears elsewhere in the book, but it serves a useful purpose to say it again. Let's see how we can grow earnings per share by using a buyback game. The XYZ Company has one thousand shares outstanding and it earns $1,000. As we can see, EPS is equal to $1 per share. Growing earnings per share the hard way involves growing profitable sales, but that takes time and risks. So the directors buy back five hundred shares and presto $1,000/500 = \$2$ per share. This is a 100 percent earnings growth based on buybacks. What happens next? The stock price goes up and the value of management's stock options goes up too.

What other ways are there to increase the value of a stock option? A gas shortage? Realize that oil is a commodity like potatoes, and that reduced supply creates an increase in price. The biggest shortage of gas comes from the bottleneck in refining capacity. Oil companies might want to find new oil supplies, but you won't see gas companies building more refineries. To build more refineries means that more gas would be supplied to the market, which means gas prices would go down. The only way to get more refinery capacity is to break up the concentration of control by monopolistic oil companies. If oil companies wanted to become profitable again, they would be better off investing in nonpolluting energy substitutes.

How about subprime mortgages? Where is the incentive to push sales of mortgages that can't be repaid? Sales bonus programs for writing mortgages that cannot be repaid are motivated by stock option compensation. These same sales push growth of EPS for companies like Countrywide.

Corporate managements justified their use of stock option compensation by the argument that they have to pay large bonuses to attract and retain high value employees. If this was an honest argument for large bonus compensation, then why didn't management use their company's earnings to pay employees? Stock options require spending hundreds of millions of dollars in company earnings to buy back stocks? Stock buy-backs are a consequence 0f issuing stock options and gift stocks. Millions of dollars in stock buy-back money could pay for a lot of bonuses. So the process is for directors of companies to issue gift stock, stock awards, and stock options to themselves and managers, cash out stockholders' money, and then buy back the stock to boost the stock's price with the money of new investors. By the way, besides dividends, the retained earnings used to buy back stocks could also be used to fund other activities such as employee wage increases, employee health care, employee retirements, and new product R and D that boosts profits just to name a few.

Another corrupt management practice is to borrow money to pay for stock buybacks. It's like borrowing money from your children's college fund to pay for expensive prostitutes. This straps the company with an interest cost that reduces cash for future investment opportunities or dividends. One way that stock prices could be propped up after the $2 trillion dollar loss suffered by stockholders in 2001 was for corporate managers to buy back their company's stocks. Money from a large number of Mom and Pop shareholders was already hollowed out by sales of gift and optioned shares. To off-set this decline in stock price support, between 2001 and 2008, corporate stock buybacks exceeded a trillion dollars. Essentially, beyond giving management insiders free stock, companies have been in the business of buying and selling their own stock. This type of activity provides an enormous incentive to game and manipulate a company's sales and earnings. Anyone interested in a sub-prime loan?

An important observation comes from Sheldon Liber ("Amazon insiders selling and stock buybacks too?" Feb. 26, 2008, www. bloggingstocks.com), who writes, "The stock buybacks are curious for several reasons: 1) it supports the stock while major insider selling is going on. 2) it implies the stock is cheap, when selling implies it is high in the view of insiders, 3) it means that management does not have a better place to invest and 4) share buybacks generally help create value for insiders holding stock options. Is it possible that management may be using shareholder money just to prop open the exit door?" Mr. Liber has seen the light! According to CNBC.COM (April 7, 2008), "Companies in the Standard & Poor 500 index bought a record $589 billion of their own stock in 2007..." No mention is made of how insiders manipulated the sale of their optioned stock for these buybacks.

THE SEC

The SEC is nothing more than a fig leaf for self-dealing by corporate management insiders and Wall Street brokers. Former Wall Street CEOs control and direct it. Their personal financial interests and the interests of their former (future) business colleagues are always at the top of their regulatory agenda. They have all the information that I have presented here and much more. The fox is truly in charge of the henhouse.

Government Oversight

I sent the three graphs, the summary analysis, and a cover letter to Representative Henry A. Waxman, California Chairman, Committee on Oversight and Government Reform, to provide the committee with an opposing view on stock option compensation. They didn't respond with a note or letter to let me know what they thought. My impression is that they conducted a sham hearing, created to placate angry investors. The committee members asked the crooks what they should do to rebuild confidence in the rip-off, short of changing the laws to prevent more skimming. Congress members don't want to damage their sweet relationship with financial contributors by asking embarrassing questions.

March 7, 2008

Representative Henry A. Waxman, California Chairman
Committee on Oversight and Government Reform

MICHAEL LA CRONE, MBA, DBA

U.S. House of Representatives
2157 Rayburn House Office Building
Washington, D.C. 20515

From: Dr. Michael R. La Crone (DBA Finance)
Burlingame, CA 94010

Today I watched a parade of CEOs explain to your committee how their stock option compensation is justified. I have enclosed a summary copy of my paper titled "Four Arguments for Why Equity Stock Options are a Fraud on the Market."

As you can see from the graphs that support my arguments, there is no way that stock option compensation can align the interests of corporate managers and shareholders. As the call option graph shows, the relationship of stock options for manages is inverse to shareholders' interest. Corporate managers are competing with shareholders for shareholders' money. Managers are skimming the funds invested by at-the-money stockholders.

Currently, corporate board members are giving themselves and CEO insiders like Charles Schwab millions of gift shares and cashing them out at shareholders' expense.

Please submit this letter and summary with graphs into the committee's testimony on executive compensation and distribute a copy of this letter with summary with graphs to the all the other committee members.

I would be happy to present a comprehensive discussion of my research at your request.

Sincerely,

Dr. Michael R. La Crone

Stock Market Reality

Essentially, Mr. Schwab is selling investors an embedded obligation to let him pay himself out of their equity funds. Between 2004 and 2006, Mr. Schwab sold over 4 million shares of "gift stock" given to him by the Board of Directors (MarketWatch.com 10-26-2006), thereby cashing out investors' ownership money. Simply, these are investors who sacrificed for hour-by-hour savings given over to larcenist by way of deception. Divide 4 million by 100= 40,000. This means that 40,000 new investors who bought 100 shares were cashed out by Mr. Schwab. You have heard of an LBO (Leveraged Buy Out), this is a LCO (Leveraged Cash Out). Assuming no other transactions, it would take 40,000 new investors to pay the same price as the first 40,000 for the first investors to get their money out at the same price. Mr. Schwab will not expose his free money gains to loss by buying his company's stock. He can get all the free stock he wants. He expects new investors to cover this pillage. Every dollar of investors' earned money taken by Mr. Schwab is unearned personal gain. In any language this is looting of investors' money by Schwab, and it is just one symptom associated with the systemically perverse activity of equity takings by thousands of corporate insiders. Wealth transfers like this are endemic to corporations and account for a significant loss to small-money mom-and-pop investors, and the 401K money of union and nonunion employees.

Capitalism and Stocks

American capitalism is built on individual economic rights. These rights include, but are not limited to, the right to private property ownership, and the right to make and enforce contracts. When mom-and-pop investors buy shares of stock, they vest the corporation's management with fiduciary power to do the corporation's business. This means that the manager has a duty to serve as a trustee for the benefit of the company's mom-and-pop shareholder owners. This trust relationship is binding as long as managers do not practice willful deceit. "Willful deceit consists of misrepresentation, concealment, or nondisclosure of material fact, or at least misleading conduct, device, or contrivance" (234 F. Supp. 201, 203). Managers must work for the benefit of owners by providing a fair exchange of value for value.

You hope that corporate managers will reinvest earnings to create a more valuable company so that you will gain price appreciation. The other possibility is that management will use the corporation as a personal piggy bank. Since managers are the gatekeepers for shareholders, they control the wealth distribution process. If the managers use their gatekeeper authority for self-dealing, then you hope you don't own that stock.

You have heard of the swindle where a con artist sells partnerships in an apartment building that is valued at $500,000, and sells fifty partnerships for $100,000 each. Well, that is similar to what happens in the stock market when a no-dividend stock sells for fifty times its book value. Hoping for price appreciation, this is what some people are buying as a stock investment. Now, imagine that these same con artists are allowed to publish the air bubble valuation of their shares in this swindle as investments and resell them to the public. That is what insiders are doing with their free or deeply discounted bonus stock. They are dumping millions of cheap or free shares, like counterfeit $100 bills so they can transfer these funds to their personal accounts. They never buy stocks because the money would be lost to some other insiders who are dumping bonus stock. Stock price is a function of the money that goes into buying the stock and supports its valuation. When "investors'" money has been drained from those investors, they can no longer afford to buy the stock and support for the stock's price falls. Schwab and management $951 million to the good and investors $951 million lost. Do you suppose that Mr. Schwab knew that what was going on? Like a burglar out the door, it was all planned in advance! There is a lot more insidious deceit, but it involves a discussion of calls and puts that are beyond the scope of this book.

Stock Fraud Business Model

Currently, the stock market is a wealth reallocation scam where insiders merely change debits into credits and credits into debits and transfer money from outsiders' pockets to insiders' pockets. In this model, the stock market is not a gamble, it is a fraud based on deception. The game is accomplished by the use of a device called a stock option, and an illusory promise to align management and shareholder interest that is not merely improbable, but is absolutely impossible to achieve. The value of an option is "derived" from the "promise" and is used as value in consideration for the exchange. This form of compensation is a sleazy, parasitic trick that allows managers to pay themselves from stockholder money instead of corporate earnings. Like milk or water contaminated by parasitic bacteria, the beneficial investment value is corrupted by a toxic device supporting freeloaders who work to destroy the investor. Congress, with the assistance of Wall Street insiders, corrupted the gatekeepers' responsibility to shareholders. Managers are using this opportunity to corrupt the equity ownership position of shareholders through wealth transfers. Here is a question for those who should answer these kinds of questions. Is buying a share of stock with an embedded option that managers can use as a compensation expense, an investment in the company's assets, or just the purchase of a company expense? Mom and Pop have enough of their own expenses without having a company shift its bonus expenses to them.

What is the difference between an asset and an expense? An asset, like cash, is stored value that can be saved, used, or sold in a value-for-value exchange. You cannot save, use, or sell an expense. An expense is a used up cost. A cost is an item of value, reduced to money that is used to produce revenue that led to profits from assets. When a cost has been expended to produce revenues, it is used up and no longer has value. It has become an expense. A stock purchase is a value-for-value exchange of money for an ownership interest in the company. When the company gives away free stock, it is giving away shareholders' ownership interest. A corporation that uses stock as a medium of exchange for management compensation has sacrificed nothing in exchange for something. An embedded option of gift or optioned stock transforms an asset into a compensation expense. The only way to recover from buying a no-value expense is to wait for the next buyer to add asset value. Without a continuous infusion of new capital, compensation options create a downward spiral of stock value.

For the purpose of adding consequence to a definition of slavery, what is the difference between taking a person's daily earnings coercively and taking a person's life savings deceptively? I believe the latter is much worse than the former. The market for those companies issuing equity stock options is a vicious cycle. It starts with new investors; management cashes out investors' equity with stock options; when investors' money is transferred to management insiders, stock price support declines driving the stock price down; management uses stock buybacks as substitute for investors' support to realign P/E ratios that attract new investors. The fraud is hidden behind free market rhetoric.

Ownership

When you buy a share of stock, you transform your 100 percent money ownership into stock ownership controlled by the discretionary will of managers. Your ownership is residual, meaning that you have a right to only what remains after all other claims against assets. Your principle and earning power depend on the discretionary wisdom of the company's board of directors. If they decide to give the managers free shares that cash you out, then it is tough luck for you. Your ownership is residual, and if the managers run the company into the ground, then it is tough luck for you. With all the risk of a company using your money to pad management insiders' accounts, and with all the accounting tricks available to insiders, it might be better to spend this kind of risk money in a casino, and keep your life's savings in the bank or buy a new car, house, or some other tangible asset. As explained earlier, a share of stock has the same characteristics as any other product. When a factory sells a product, the product is sold new, and the factory gets the money, but once the product has been sold to the public, then the product is no longer new; it is used and is sold as used in a secondary market. When a share of stock is sold new in the primary (IPO) market, the company gets the money. When a share of stock is sold again in the secondary market, like a used refrigerator, the share is sold as used and the company gets no money. Brokers and dealers make a market in these used stocks and the proceeds from sales go to the brokers and dealers (and some fast traders) who sell them. If they cash out at the right time, long-term "investors" are lucky to capture a price gain from inflation.

A share's value depends on the honesty and integrity of the brokers or dealers who make a market trafficking in the asserted value of paper claims. Investing in an assertion of value made by someone who has lied for personal gain as opposed to investing in a real value-for-value exchange is like paying for a counterfeit ticket to a football game. You have been sold a pig in a poke with deceptive information ("investing" in "asserts" not assets). Equity options provide self-dealing personal gain as an incentive for stock dealers and other insiders to lie. Mr. Schwab had an incentive to lie for over $400,000,000 in personal gain that he took out of mom-and-pop savings from their retirement stock investments. Of course, Mr. Schwab is hoping that they won't miss it until they are ready to retire and by then no one will know where the money went. If a dealer tells you a share is selling for $5, then that is the price the dealer has put on it. This price need not have a relationship to any underlying market value. Is this an "investment" that Mom and Pop should rely on for their retirement? Until there are laws that provide honest accounting for underlying value, where buyers are protected by 100 percent ownership rights, and insiders are punished for self-dealing wealth transfers, it might be more profitable buying and selling used refrigerators, or toasters, as scrap metal; at least there is a real market for valuing scrap metal. Let the weeds grow over Wall Street's sale of paper claims, and buy an asset that you own 100 percent.

Tricks

Many of the tricks used by Enron to subvert stockholders' equity positions are still alive, and are being used by other companies in 2009. Beyond the stupidity of Enron executives to believe that they could get away with cooking the books, there were many great opportunities to rip off investors without cooking the books. Enron's management had a huge source of unearned wealth available to them through stock options. Stock options, as will be covered in later pages, pervert the matching process of revenues to expenses by stealing money from investors' equity to pay company compensation expenses. Revenues are overstated and expenses understated by taking shareholders' money, in the form of deeply discounted stock, to pay the company's management compensation. All the insider gains are then reported as a corporate compensation expense—even though the corporation used none of its earnings. Consequently, reduced compensation expenses distort real earnings. The company gets free labor, management gets free money, and the mom-and-pop stock investors get screwed. Equity stock options are a riskless gain to management insiders and a certain deadweight loss to stock investing outsiders. Ask Schwab if he will make the same option alignment deal with his gardener. As a bonus, he gives his gardener equity in his home for doing a better gardening job. The gardener would soon have a new residence.

Another deception used by management to increase their personal gains at stockholders' expense is to use earnings that would be available for dividends to buy back the company's stock. Buying back the company's stock reduces the number of shares outstanding and creates a stock price performance illusion that the company's earnings are a favorable indicator of its stock value. To obtain short-term earnings gains that will boost the stock price and stock option gains, managers can hollow out the company by diverting research and development funds, reducing expenses for maintenance, and shrinking funding for new products or new market development that would grow the company's revenues. Recently, many companies have borrowed money to buy back their shares. A prelude of what might be in the future was an announcement by Pfizer (The Associated Press, Jan. 22, 2007, at http://dailynews. att.net) that they are laying off ten thousand employees to cut costs; and that Motorola (USA Today Jan. 19, 2007, at http://usatoday. com) will cut thirty-five hundred jobs to improve operating costs. Earnings that could be used for employment are being diverted for stock buybacks to boost stock prices and stock option gains. Executives in both these companies have cashed out millions of dollars in gift and optioned stock shares. Equity options undermine the legitimacy of paid-in owners' equity, as well as the stock ownership position of new-to-the-market investors. Wall Street and management insiders are sticking a financial needle into the arm of labor and bleeding its earned retirement wealth with the help of Wall Street's President George W. Bush and select members of the finance committee from both political parties in Congress. For an excellent discussion on the accounting treatment of stock option gains and how Microsoft and other corporations lie to investors see; Profits You Can Trust by H. D. Sherman, S. D. Young, and H. Collingwood (FT Prentice Hall, 2003, p.140). Two other important books about how Wall Street and management insiders work are Pump and Dump by R. H. Tillman and Michael L. Indergaard (Rutgers University Press, 2005), and Origins of the Crash by Roger Lowenstein (The Penguin Press, 2004).

Corruption

Even though the stock market is only a segment of finance in the American economy, without an iota of exaggeration it is just as corrupt, deceitful, counterfeit, and rotten as the financial system of any Third World dictatorship. And it might take the same amount of national determination to correct it. Whether it was Hitler stealing hard-earned money from German Jews during WW II—or Gary Winnick,2 with Jewish family roots in war-torn Europe, who controlled Global Crossing, stealing over a billion dollars in stockholders' money from WW II veterans, their widows and children, and veterans who gave life and limb to save German Jews from certain death—or Mr. Schwab freeloading on stockholders' equity—they all share in the same crime of stealing retirement savings from the moms and pops who earned it or stealing from the widows and orphans who inherited it from the moms and pops who earned it. Jews are still trying to get back over a billion dollars of what was stolen from them during Hitler's war. It should not take as long for victims of Wall Street's embezzlement of 2000–2001 to get their money returned. As a Jew, Winnick cannot insulate himself from such a harsh assessment of his parasitic theft by hiding behind the pain of real Holocaust victims. Stealing from Jews and stealing from veterans is a valid comparison of flagrant financial misdeeds that may have life-and-death consequences. Certainly, this assessment is not meant to be a comparison of the egregious life-and-death misdeeds of Hitler; there is no intention to trivialize the suffering of those Jews and solders who lived and died under Hitler with a comparison to Winnick's financial "killings." Wall Street apologists can quibble about how much and why, but the facts remain—corrupt parasitic self-dealers like Schwab and Winnick stole over a billion dollars in equity from mom-and-pop earnings through stock option and gift stock wealth transfers. You might be tempted to be academically polite with these people, but if you are polite, they will brush you off like a bad case of dandruff. Your grandmother, with the loss of her stock investment retirement funds, could be tossed into the street because of their actions, but, as long as you didn't point the finger at them, they would not care. They don't care how many people point fingers at them. They're beyond feeling any shame or even embarrassment.

The most important message conveyed in this book is that stock compensation bonuses are theft. The wealth of shareholders is being looted by stock brokers and corporate management insiders through the use of device (stock options and gift stock), and deceit. Corporate boards are using freeloaded gift stocks to selectively skim money out of shareholders' purchased shares at top-of-the-market prices. Their authority was engineered by political manipulation and their legitimacy gained by deceit and lies. Neither the Securities and Exchange Commission nor the Terms and Conditions of shareholders' equity ownership rights have prevented corporate boards from self-dealing predations of shareholders' equity.

Symptomatic of insiders' corrupt self-dealing in stocks is the vicious fraud on Mom and Pop investors by the management of General Electric. Reported in the New York Times, Aug. 5th 2009, General Electric Corporation has been fined by the Securities and Exchange Commission $50 million for manipulating earnings between 2002 and2003. GE Managers were incentivized to manipulate earnings to maximize their gains on gift and optioned shares of stock. Because the corporation will pay the fine, investors are victimized twice. Also symptomatic is the bought-off and sold-out political system where congressional investigators either ignore the corrupt practices of corporate managers or they give them a tongue lashing and admonishes them not to do it again. None of the now wealthy executives who committed fraudulent manipulation of stock prices for personal gain will face a court of justice. Mom and Pop, who lost their life's savings, will forever be victims of felonious crimes ignored and justice denied.

All financial assets are the result of translating abstract formulas into products. These financial formulas are constrained by terms and conditions. Unlike physical assets that can be comprehended, understood, and appreciated by the senses of taste, touch, sight, hearing, and smell; financial assets are abstract and intangible. All financial assets are a collection of promises enhanced by an Intermediator's value added service of promising asset owners financial benefits that fill financial needs. The only way a financial asset can be understood is through the information given to the asset owner by an Intermediator bank or broker who manages the asset's ownership value.

Trust between Intermediators and asset owners govern all financial relationship. In the news recently, Bernard Madoff was given 150 years in federal prison for running an investment ponzi that cost investors, including charities, widows, and Mom and Pop retirements $50 billion. Previous to getting caught, he held a high ranking position as a non-executive chairman of the NASDAQ stock exchange. He knew the rules and the risks, and still had little concern for his victims. A Madoff limerick has been added in the new material at the end of the book. Madoff's theft is small compared to what is being taken by corporate insiders through self-dealing in gift stocks.

I have a data set showing that twenty-five executives from five corporations have received over 102 million gift shares. Multiply just this small sample of shares times $50, and you get a sense of the real stock market ponzi theft. Compared to the deceit, lies, and opaquely disclosed self-dealing by stock brokers and corporate managers Bernard Madoff's theft is a petty crime. This is déjà vu 1929.President Obama and Congress has swallowed Wall Street's Cool Aid, and support burying this monumental theft under a mountain of bank bailout and recession recovery money.

Defined in economic terms, taking retirement money from Mom and Pop through deception and device is analogous to treating mom and pop like a herd of livestock working them all their lives and compensating them , as a herd, with only the benefit of food and shelter; while those in control take for themselves the surplus of the herd's production. Read the history of company towns in America (Google), the economics are similar and the results are the same. This is a stealth form of slavery. Sounds a little Marxist, but I believe in market driven capitalism over any current form of socialism. Marx was absolutely wrong to accuse capitalism as being unjust. The injustice associated with capitalism and socialism stems from the deception and self-dealing of those in control of managing the earnings and savings of labor.

I use the words parasite and parasitic in the text repeatedly. The purpose of reiterating these words is to underline the insidious, malicious, and destructive nature of insiders' crimes against a trusting public. Have no doubt, this book exposes a pernicious financial war conducted by Wall Street power brokers, stock brokers, and corporate managers who have carte blanche privileged authority to treat investors' money as a personal entitlement.

Government by Insiders and for Insiders

One of the biggest mistakes you can make as a stock "investor" is to think that there is an agency of government that will protect you from insider fraud. The U.S. Securities and Exchange

Commission attempts to create a sense of regulatory integrity over the stock market by requiring companies to disclose their earnings, but executives simply lie in their disclosures to boost stock prices and their options, cash out investors' equity, and then file a restatement of earnings.

Even without the deceptive disclosures, stock options are still a huge rip-off. Deceptive disclosures, like backdating grant dates to increase an option's value, just increase the losses. Stock market regulation by financial disclosure is absolutely worthless for protecting investors from predatory management. There is no market failure in this snake oil treachery; it is a failure of government oversight and the rule of law to protect the public. This failure of trust and duty is the consequence of a sellout by government insiders to Wall Street interest. Agencies of government that are supposed to protect you have been preempted by the corrupting influence of big money lobbying and the opportunity for cushy jobs from Wall Street. That is how Wall Street insiders get away with so much without being sent to prison.

Another layer of corruption arises from Wall Street's use of campaign money to buy influence with the president and Congress for insider jobs as commissioners in the Securities and Exchange Commission. Harvey Pitt, a Wall Street attorney who was appointed as chief of the SEC, is a good example. Appointing Harvey Pitt to command the SEC was like appointing a Mafia lawyer to lead the FBI. Placing Pitt in a position that allowed him to be the judge of his friends and future employers was a conflict of interest and should not have been tolerated. But President George W. Bush, who appointed him, found Pitt an expedient tool to serve the interest of Wall Street and, of course, to serve his own interests.

Like former president George W. Bush, his father, George H. W. Bush, was also a beneficiary of Wall Street money. Bush sold out the public's interest and betrayed those who voted for him. Wall Street insiders have President Bush in their pocket. Wall Street insiders refer to Bush as the world's most powerful scam-monkey that Wall Street has ever employed. I am glad Bush wasn't in the potato business, or else French fries would be $5 a bag. Come to think of it, he and his friends in oil might still have the power to drive up diesel fuel costs to where French fries will cost $5. If I were president, I would investigate Bush, top Wall Street executives, and top oil company executives for financial crimes against America. The Federal Reserve's Alan Greenspan and predecessor Ben Bernanke have aligned themselves with Wall Street insiders in a transparent arbitrage play by reducing interest rates to weaken the dollar and drive up commodity prices including oil prices. This illustrates the level of insider self-dealing within the ranks of government. The idea that growing world demand is driving up oil prices is not credible when China is paying $70 a barrel for oil at the same time that the United States is paying $100 a barrel. This is price manipulation and it is not coming from OPEC; it's coming from American oil companies aligned with Wall Street's ability to manipulate markets with its financial muscle and creative derivative devices.

As a side note, what was Bush doing to fight terrorism besides killing and injuring a lot of men, women, and children? Ask the average Iraqi what he thinks of the United States killing innocent men, women, and children, and he will respond, "Thanks, we needed Mr. Bush to teach us a lesson of what America is all about." Where is the flea Osama bin Laden that Bush was supposed to bring to justice? The Bush family and the bin Laden family are close friends—maybe too close. Osama is not in Iraq, that is for certain. Another certainty is that Bush is rearranging the cash flows in Iraq to benefit his oil friends and insiders on Wall Street.

Congress too, both Democrats and Republicans, have sold out to let Wall Street interests come before serving the interests of public justice. Between tax rip-offs of self-dealing red-ink Democrats and lying Wall Street-connected rip-offs of self-dealing Republicans; the working poor and middle class have been swindled for too long, it's time for change. You need not look too far to find evidence that representative government is safely tucked into the wallet of Wall Street and the bank accounts of Washington insiders. David Kirkpatrick, (www.nytimes.com/2007/01/23writing in The New York Times in January 22, 2007, article titled "Death Knell May Be Near For Public Election Funds," says that Hillary Clinton will "forgo public financing...because of the spending limits that come with the federal money." Clinton is "confident she could raise far more than the roughly $150 million the system would provide..." "...Clinton was merely confirming what many in Washington already knew: that the public financing system has failed to keep pace with the torrents of money flowing toward the presidential elections." Bush received over $270 million in private donations. What do you suppose $270 million bought from Mr. Bush? It wasn't merely tea in the Rose Garden.

Hedge Funds

Two of the most important news stories that no one followed for their stock market relevance have to do with public officials quitting their jobs to run hedge funds. Reported by Rob Cox, David Vise, and Dwight Cass in the Wall Street Journal (March 31, 2007, B14, Mr. Richard Breeden, former SEC chairman, quit his job at the SEC to run a hedge fund. Reports are that he doesn't know a thing about finance needed to run a hedge fund, but he is an expert at not getting caught. Bloomberg news reported on April 27, 2008, that Ms. Christianna Wood quit her job as senior investment officer at California Public Employees' Retirement System (CalPERS) to become CEO of the hedge fund Capital Z Asset Management capital. What makes this important news for stock investors? To answer that question, you need to know a little about hedge funds.

Hedge funds are unregulated private equity mutual funds, that is, they have large amounts of capital that can be invested in the stock market without a set of laws of public responsibility and without being supervised or tracked by regulators. Wall Street uses the Wild West metaphor to describe hedge funds, but a more appropriate metaphor is swine flu. Hedge funds act most often like a pernicious virus infecting healthy capital markets. The implications are disturbing. With a large block of capital, hedge funds can pump and dump a company's shares. Wealthy bankers formulated the pump-and-dump process in the 1920s when they formed trusts. They used blocks of capital to buy a stock that had some market cachet such as General Electric to create price momentum. As public investors started buying the stock on the momentum, the trust would short the stock, taking investor money support for the stock down. This is a volatility strategy. For management insiders and hedge fund operators the stock market is not an investment, it is a pouch bowl, and they are going to drain as much punch out of the bowl as they can before the host takes the bowl away.

After a corporation sells its stock to capitalize its operational existence with the issuance of stock in an initial public offering, dealers and investors are allowed to sell these IPO shares in a secondary market. This secondary market for stocks is a little like selling used underwear. This means that the company does not get any money in the transaction. Stock transactions in a secondary market are strictly zero-sum exchanges between sellers who would rather have the money and buyers who think that the stock has some exchange value. The problem with management gift stock and stock options transactions are that they exchange no cost paper for investors' real money.

Here is how hedge funds hedge investors out of investors' investments. Hedge fund stock transactions are a rip-off within a rip-off. Hedge fund managers find top-rated companies whose stock seems to be undervalued by the market. The key is to find investors seeking yield through a stock's earnings growth momentum or investors trying to find stock price growth in a low earnings environment. Usually, this is a company where management insiders have been using free shares or option shares to bleed investors and the investors have lost so much equity that they drop out of the market; fewer investors for the company's shares means lower share price. Next, the hedge team will buy cheap call and put options on the stock. This is a part of the hedge. Then the hedge team buys the stock just before an earnings report. Stock sales get a boost on good earnings reports and on good stories about a company with a poor earnings report. A hedge fund invests large blocks of funds, driving up share price and creating buyer momentum. When the stock's price hits a certain number, they cash in their calls, short the stock and sell their long shares. The momentum is reversed, driving stock prices down. A short sale is where you sell high, and buy low, expecting (helping) the stock price to drop. The hedgers buy back the shares at a low price and return the stock used in their short sale.

Finally, after the stock price drops, they cash out their put options and the deal is complete. It is an almost riskless manipulation. The result is shareholders' capital shrinks. The question is did Christianna Wood, a public employee, collude with hedge funds to boost CalPERS' returns? Did she use hedge fund tactics to boost CalPERS' returns? Did Mr. Breeden use his position to influence the SEC's regulatory position on stock compensation for management insiders?

WORDS

How do people get caught up in the scams of Wall Street? Besides the critical purpose of financing America's businesses, Wall Street's purpose is to provide the functional utility of a financial institution which serves the public's financing needs through a fiduciary (trust) relationship. These financial institutions are the domain of individual decision makers and their power over the use and abuse of their position power.

Two features of position power connect those with authority to those impacted by authority. The rhetoric of power and the power of rhetoric can be placed on a continuum from benign self-interested paternalism to pernicious self-dealing egoism. Mr. Schwab and Wall Street's upper management are on the polar end of pernicious egoism. For Mr. Schwab and Wall Street, the rhetoric of power is lying, and the power of rhetoric is a compelling lie. Those who control information material to making decisions concerning the public's financial activities use the tools of abstraction to gloss over abuses of their decision authority. This is the rhetoric of power.

There are too many examples to list, but here is one. Earnings per share are the numbers that drive stock purchases. Let's see how we can grow earnings per share the easy way by using a buyback game. The XYZ Company has one thousand shares outstanding and it earns $1,000. As we can see, EPS is equal to $1 per share. Growing earnings per share the hard way involves growing profitable sales, but that takes time and risks. So the directors buy back five hundred shares and presto, $1,000/500 = $2 per share. This is a 100 percent earnings growth based on buybacks. What happens next? The stock price goes up and the value of management's stock options goes up too. Mom and Pop buy the stock and insiders skim the money right off the top.

The power of rhetoric is the ability to create a perception of reality from a compelling lie. H. A. Simon said that "Any rational decision may be viewed as a conclusion reached from certain premises...The behavior of a rational person can be controlled, therefore, if the value and the factual premises upon which he bases his decisions are specified for him." H. A. Simon (1944), "Decision Making and Administrative Organization," Public Administration Review.

This approach of scripting reality to mold behavior has been used by Communist China and Russia, Hollywood, Wall Street, President Bush, and Charles Schwab to engender public trust. This is obviously a short list of candidates just to give you a sense of the power of political rhetoric...They carefully package their words with omissions and half-truths to create belief. Snake oil salesmen say, "Buy this tonic and it will cure your lumbago." Stock dealers say, "Buy this stock, it's an investment." Politicians say, "Vote for me. I'll help you."

Those in Congress who control the legislative agenda dedicate themselves to creating economic problems and curing the symptoms caused by the problems they have created. They create the problem and become the solution. Why? Because that is how to make money in politics!

Words, like parasite and self-dealer, frequently used in this book to describe people or their actions may seem impolite or insensitive, but they have been carefully selected to describe exactly the character of people and actions discussed. There are no value judgments or moral dimensions to the descriptions of these characters and their actions; these are only descriptions, like a worm in the apple, representing states of nature.

The stealth and predatory nature of Mr. Schwab's unearned wealth transfers; coupled with his cold calculating indifference to those who suffered unjustifiable losses, merits him the characterization of a financial parasite. Schwab could not be happy with being a multimillionaire; he had to steal shareholders' equity to become a billionaire.

Not even an individual with a graduate education in finance had the academic background needed to recognize the self-dealing2 conflicts of interests that have been the hallmark of this continuing stock market rip-off. Only insiders had the necessary information needed to deal with the complexity and difficulty of Wall Street's word meanings and concept interpretations. Insiders like selected members in Congress, such as Sen. Joseph Lieberman; connected judges; ex-senators, like Phil Gramm; and ex-SEC attorneys like Harvey Pitt, Stephen Cutler, and William McLucas, who found that their service to the public could be used for lucrative personal gain3 serving the private interests of Wall St. and million dollar Wall Street attorneys; and favored compensation consultants, who serve as purveyors for the counterfeit interests of boards and managers had the inside information. However, they seem to believe that if they could fool the public, then all would be well with the world.

BLAME THE VICTIM

Educators are taught not to blame the student for expressing harmful or naïve ideas, but to attack the ideas, showing how and why the ideas are harmful or naïve. Self-dealing insiders, ignoring or perhaps deflecting their own accountability, will always resort to blaming the cupidity of victims. They will blame the investor for being greedy, for trying to get something for nothing, lack of attention to details, etc.

Consequently, in the case of self-dealers this caveat against blaming the person does not apply; within the law or not, self-dealing is equivalent to intentional theft. Mr. Schwab blamed investors for being "immature investors" and for their failure to diversify. In an interview, Charles Fishman4 asks Mr. Charles Schwab what an investor should do in a bear market. Schwab answers "...The worst thing you can do is not be in the market." This comment is a vague reference to the idea that investor money is safe from the deceptive wealth transfers of corporate managers. It borders on criminally misleading advice to investors. He doesn't let on that investors are losing their life savings to corporate managers like him through equity skimming. In another part of this article, Schwab describes all those who lost their money as "immature investor(s)" versus the "sage investor" such as himself. He doesn't let on that he is transferring hundreds of millions dollars of stockholders' wealth into his own account.

When asked what Mr. Schwab thought about how investors were dealing with their losses in this economic downturn, Schwab says, "Quite well." He says that only about 5% of investors were hurt by the current downturn, "the technology investors that were not diversified!" "Most people in their 401(k) s are diversified. Here at Schwab, they are reasonably diversified—they've been coached to be." He is implying that without his coaching that ignorant investors deserve the loss of their retirement savings. What he leaves out is that diversification merely minimizes the impact of the market's decline. Diversification hides the wealth transfer taken by insiders from a few stocks in a portfolio of stocks where some of them are honestly valued.

Fishman says to Schwab, "You've preached financial independence, yet some of your customers have lost 20% of what they had a year ago." Mr. Schwab parades his haughty arrogance by responding "True. But 15% to 20% is a modest reduction given the reward one gets by being a successful, sage, long term investor." In other words, he is saying that the most recently invested money is gone and stockholders will have to wait for future stockholders' money to get their money back. He suggests that the thousands of "immature investors" who lost all their retirements saving are just part of ups and downs of owning stock, and that their loss has nothing to do with self-dealing manipulations of parasitic insiders like him.

HISTORY DÉJÀ VU

The view of this article is that history is repeating itself like the Wall Street stock market rip-off of 1929;5 corporate managers and Wall Street insiders are looting stockholders' investments. During the 1929 Depression, equity options were, through manipulations and deceptions, scandalously used by bank boards and management insiders for self-enrichment, and brought about multimillion-dollar wealth transfers from office workers, policemen, and farmers earning $25 a week. With an annual income of $1,300 a year, these $25 a week wages, on average, supported a 3 percent annual savings rate of $39. Houses sold for less than $2,000, cars for less than $500, and jobs were plentiful. Wall Street financial parasites drained the pool of mom and pop's purchasing power, and the economy took a dive. Macroeconomic analysis suggesting tight credit and monetary policy as a contributing cause of the Depression missed the point. Loose credit and easy money would not have stopped the loss of savings needed by consumers to sustain the production side of the economy. The Depression stopped wealth transfers when there was no more money to lose and no hope for the money lost. In the aftermath of 2000–2001, President Bush and Alan Greenspan were well aware of the need to increase government spending by increasing the national debt, and cutting taxes to keep the economy from going into a downward spiral.

The same management equity option incentive rationale used then is being used now. A recent article in the San Jose Mercury News6 tells how eBay Chief Operating Officer Maynard Webb took $90 million in equity stock option7 gains between 1999 and 2006. Since he has cleaned out $90 million of investors' retirement money, he has decided to retire. At $12,857,142 a year, he has scored big on the backs of unsuspecting investors. Especially from those investors who have their money in managed retirement accounts. He is just one of many insiders taking advantage of free money gifts from their corporate boards, who are, of course, giving themselves free money bonuses. One scenario is that when new investors get wise to this stock market rat hole, they won't put their money up for grabs, and market prices will fall. Corporations will prop up stock prices for a while through stock repurchases, but in the end, the taxpayer will be enlisted to replace losses. Congress will see to it that investors are repaid pennies for the loss of their dollars by taxes on the investors' wages. Those who took the money will keep it, and preach the virtues of hard work, saving, sacrifice, and long-term stocks.

BUBBLE BULL

Many investors new to the stock market in 2000–2001 suffered substantial losses of equity. The standard explanation describes their loss as a "market bubble" implying that stocks were over priced and they were caught in the selloff.

This paper considers the impact of management compensation through the device of equity stock options on shareholders' wealth. The rationale of aligning management and shareholders' interest with equity stock options, or any other equity device that transfers shareholders' wealth, is fatally flawed. Compensating management by means of equity options is a zero-sum8 self-dealing wealth transfer that has an inverse relationship to the interests of new-to-the-market investors who buy at top-of-the- market prices. Equity stock options create a skimming process of shareholders' wealth where management takes an arbitrage gain through a one-sided options transaction. New-to-the-market investors are at-the-money,9 but within an instant, Mr. Schwab's cash-out of his equity options bleeds equity support for the stock price, and new investors are forced out of the money. Market bidding has little to do with this stock price decline. Investors in 2000–2001 who bought option-embedded stock exercised by management were not sold an investment, but merely a management compensation expense. There was no risk/return investment; there was only a bookkeeping entry to execute a wealth transfer.

SCHWAB AS EMBLEM

Although Mr. Charles Schwab and his management are used in this summary as a case study in skimming shareholders' money through equity stock options, the practice is today viral, and widely used by many companies. The reasons I chose Mr. Schwab for this spotlight are (1) Mr. Schwab knew exactly how his equity skimming would impact new investors, but ignored their losses for his own personal gain. (2) Mr. Schwab and his management are gatekeepers of their investors' money. When a gatekeeper sells out his trust and loyalty for personal gain, it needs to be exposed. (3) The idea of objective board members in a disinterested compensation committee approving arm's-length multimillion-dollar bonuses to themselves and management is a delusional fiction. (4) The SEC is an enormous informational haystack that creates the illusion of investor information. Millions of pages of companies' disclosure filings are accessible to only a few people with skills necessary for efficient and effective research. Buried information, transparent or deceptive, amounts to no information. (5) The SEC failed to protect long-term investors from the predations of management insiders.

An equity stock option is a pernicious device for skimming investor equity that encourages predatory management activity for the purpose of transferring investors' wealth to management as unearned personal gain. In a world of $12 per hour labor and $4 a pound chicken, the bonus money of $951 million (Fortune, Sept. 2, 2002) given to Mr. Schwab and his managers is a lot to lose for mom-and-pop investors. The indulgence appetite for money of Mr. Schwab and his management by taking gains from the unsuspecting public, created huge losses that collapsed many individual retirement accounts, and shrunk the retirement funds of all investors. Mr. Schwab, along with other billionaire and multimillionaire CEOs, who have taken monumental amounts of investor money, have contributed greatly to the impoverished retirements of moms and pops who placed their trust in him. Schwab's credit extension functions to margin accounts only compounded investors' losses.

Fortune (Sept. 2, 2002) listed Mr. Schwab as one of the greediest executives in America, but until now, no one questioned his actions as anything more than excessive. If you learn something new about Mr. Schwab and his management concerning how you lost your money in the stock market from this paper, consider it the disclosure you didn't get when you bought your stocks.

Equity Stock Compensation is a Form of Equity Skimming:
Or How to Turn a Shareholder's Ownership Account into
A Manager's Bonus Account with Equity Stock Options10

This paper challenges as fatally flawed the accepted rationale that equity stock options are an appropriate compensation incentive device for corporate management and employees. This challenge applies equally to all other forms of option-like equity compensation schemes that transfer shareholders' wealth.

The process of transferring wealth from investors to managers through the device of equity options in exchange for the consideration of fulfilling some future promise to improve the wealth of shareholders by managers is on its face an empty pledge. The logic of using equity incentive compensation as a way to compete for management talent is deceptive, manipulative, and self-serving. Exposing an investor's equity ownership account to wealth transfer is financially irrational. Motives for equity options that claim to align management interest with shareholders' interest do not qualify as justification.

The real meaning of equity option wealth transfer is that corporations have been given congressional power to use a manipulative device for stock market transactions. Equity options provide management with a free-riding subsidy that sanctions an exchange of real wealth from shareholders' equity ownership for the consideration of illusory promises and hypothesized opinions about management motivation.

THE PROBLEM

Investing in a corporation's stock is a risk/return asset allocation decision. Stock equity ownership is a long-term investment in a corporation's assets used to produce financial returns over time. Suppose Mom and Pop decide to sell their home and live off the accumulated equity. They move into a retirement apartment and decide to follow the advice in a local stock dealer's book on how to invest. They put 25 percent of their $200,000 in savings into the bank as a drawing account and the rest into a portfolio of technology (growth) stocks and the stock of the stock dealer's company. Within five months, they lose 90 percent of their "investment." Much later, they find out that managers in these corporations were cashing out billions of dollars from the equity of stock investors' accounts for pennies on the dollar through equity stock options. Ninety percent of their money was wiped out and their "investment" permanently impaired. This is a scenario that played out in real terms for many shareholders in the 2000–2001 stock market. What happened to their nest egg?

Equity option compensation is not paid by the corporation; it is a liquidation of shareholders' interest by management and for management. Compensation is no longer tied to a company's revenues; it has been morphed into a game where management competes with investors for investors' money. Like a welfare device, equity (stock) options redistribute equity from investor to compensation for management in a zero-sum transaction without an exchange of material value. Investors are not buying the net realizable value of assets and they are not paying for liabilities to be turned into profits; there is no investment or return for investors, but merely a wealth transfer for a bonus expense. Equity options turn an investor's equity ownership account into a management compensation account. This wealth transfer is not a corporation's expense, but an investor's permanent loss. You can own an asset, but you cannot own an expense. Buying a compensation expense is buying a used up cost, there is no return on investment. Once an expense is paid, the money is gone. An equity option transaction creates a free-money zero-risk gain for management. Rather than aligning the interest of managers with shareholders, compensating managers with equity gift and option stock have an inverse alignment that promotes a strong motivation for management to grow more risk-free money at the expense of investors.

CORPORATE BENEFITS

Besides receiving favorable tax treatment, equity options benefit a corporation two ways. First, it receives a compensation and bonus subsidy from shareholders that reduce its labor expense. This improves profit margins. Second, the corporation benefits from the premium it receives by writing options for managers. This improves revenue margins. Recently, the business news has exposed the practice of corporations buying back their stock. One purpose of stock repurchases is to artificially maintain market prices for a company's stock while managers convert their options into cash. Compensation is supposed to be a corporation's responsibility, and it is supposed to be paid out of revenues. When a company's revenues are insufficient to pay expenses, then compensation should come from a corporation's capital account—never from investors' ownership equity accounts. Rather than aligning the corporation's interest with the shareholder, corporations have a short-term incentive to align their interest with management. Research studying the interaction between market forces and changes of a company's stock price has not tested the effects of equity options on shareholders' returns for new-to-the-market at-the-money investors. Skimming equity from new-to-the-market investors who buy shares at a top-of-the-market stock price does not have the same effect on equity as those who are early to the market deep-in-the-money investors. They are not the same investors. Wealth is being transferred from one and not the other.

The rationale of this discussion is to show that promises to improve a company's stock price for the right of managers to transfer shareholders' wealth through risk-free transactions cannot benefit public investors. Logically, an option transaction will graphically show that there is an absolute inverse relationship between investors' wealth and management's equity option gains. As a result, investors' money is skimmed from stocks, leaving most recent investors to divide their loss.

MARKET DIFFERENCES

Before one can understand what goes on in the stock market, a distinction must be made between a pre initial public offering (pre IPO), and a post initial public offering (post IPO). There are two markets for stocks. In the pre IPO stage, owners distribute founder's shares that will later be exchanged for public shares. There is the primary market where IPO stocks are issued to owners, employees, managers, venture capitalists, vendors, lawyers, accountants, and anyone else who can exchange services for a share in the company. Here is where owners take some percentage of the IPO shares' distribution that will amount to a majority ownership stake. If the corporation issues one hundred thousand shares, then the owners will want to issue to themselves shares that provide a majority interest. Government regulates what percentage of equity is allowed to be distributed. There is nothing wrong with this arrangement; they deserve their controlling ownership shares of the company. Money received from the issue of IPO stocks is paid to the company as capital for the company to fund operational activities and invest in assets.

Next, there is the secondary market where shares issued to IPO investors are sold to public investors. Here is where the stock dealer makes money. The stock dealer takes what amounts to used stocks, and, like a used car dealer, sells these used stocks to the public. The corporation does not receive any of the money from secondary stocks being traded. Stock dealers, just as used car dealers, often trade for their own account if they can make a gain on the deal. Trillions of dollars in used stocks in the secondary market with equity options embedded in them are being sold and billions of dollars have and are still being taken out through equity options. What stock dealers are not telling mom-and-pop investors is the illusory value exchanged for their "investment" money and that equity options are nothing less than a back door wealth transfer device.

PURPOSE OF A SECONDARY MARKET

How did a secondary market in stocks develop and why does it exist? Like a person who owns a large tract of land and wants to diversify risk and returns to real assets by selling some of it for cattle, so the secondary market for stocks developed naturally as a consequence of stock owners' desires to diversify their risks and returns in financial assets by buying bonds and selling some of their stocks.

Secondary markets are supposed to distribute the risk and rewards of ownership. Wide distribution of earned ownership of corporate assets by labor undermined the Marxist critique of capitalism that monopolists exploit workers through self-dealing. Labor becomes the owners of the means of production without the help of a proletariat dictatorship. Markets, and not the command and control of government planners, become the determinate of what to produce, by whom, for whom, and at what price. The current self-dealing by corporate managers and Wall Street insiders undermines the concept of earned ownership of the means of production.

Marxists concerned themselves with the corrupt behavior of corporate monopolies by condemning the disenfranchisement and exploitation of an individual's labor. To overcome the corrupt corporation, the Marxist leaders remove corrupt corporate managers and substitute them with corrupt politicians in government monopolies. All monopolies, political or corporate, are prone to corruption. When those in charge of monopolistic power exploit the earnings and savings of a helpless individual for their personal financial gain or political power, they should be punished and striped of their wealth and power. Wall Street managers, oil company executives, and powerful politicians like Bush are living high on the hog of corrupt practices while day labor and honest corporate managers are being sold a pig in a poke.

SECONDARY MARKETS

There is an important difference between aligning the interests of owners, managers, employees, etc…before the stock is traded on the secondary market and after it is traded on the secondary market. The interest of pre IPO owners, managers, and employees is to maximize their gains from issuing stock to the public. The interest of those selling their IPO stock is to maximize their gains. Distribution of equity options through the IPO process is a dilution of the public shareholder's investment, and is justified by the rationale that a corporation may become more valuable than the owners anticipated. From a financial point of view, there is no risk/return tradeoff in an equity option transaction, but simply a wealth transfer. Giving an equity option to management after the stock has passed into the secondary market makes no sense and has no defense. Most investors do not put their money in companies to have it become an ATM for management. Imagine if all investors were rolled into just one investor losing a billion dollars in two years to management bonus compensation transfers; a court action would soon follow.

ILLUSORY PROMISES

Textbooks and stock promoters will tell you that there is an exchange going on between managers and shareholders. Managers are exchanging a promise for shareholders' money. They will tell you that equity options are a compensation device used to motivate and reward management and employees. Somehow, it is rationalized; managers and employees will align their interests more closely with shareholders if they are given the opportunity to cash out shareholders' investments. A hollow proposition, but it has worked for insiders so far.

This creates a comforting illusion that managers are receiving earned compensation for their work, just like Mom and Pop!. It can be shown that the idea of alignment between management's and shareholders' interests is based on an illusory promise, and it follows that the promise by management is not an exchange of value, but merely the use of a lie that legitimates a device for transferring investors' wealth. If there is use of a device (equity stock options) and an illusory promise, then one can deduce that there is fraud on the market.

DEFERRED COMPENSATION

The underlying principle of option compensation has been perverted by the misinterpretation of its purpose. Equity options were supposed to be a method used by start-up companies for aligning the interest of pre IPO company management and employees when cash was scarce. Giving employees a piece of the company was supposed to act as an incentive intended for high value employees to work in a cash strapped start-up that could afford little or no monetary compensation. Corporate compensation would be paid to employees when the business became profitable.

Public companies are supposed to fund their compensation expenses out of corporate earnings. It is irrational for shareholders' equity to provide the source of that compensation. In 2000–2001, many new stock investors believed that corporations paid their managers compensation out of the revenues generated from the corporation's operating, financial, and investment activities. Many investors still believe that somehow corporations pay for equity "stock" options.

PIRATE SIGNALS

Dividends and stock price appreciation are two ways that a corporation signals the market that share value has substance and that the company is growing in value. Many investors are looking for company growth through earnings or acquisitions and the consequent stock price appreciation. For companies that are trying to grow their stock price, the dividend signal for income is traded off for the growth signal through corporate acquisitions.

Equity option compensation, as a skimming process, is in reality a pirate's incentive to corrupt market signals for self-dealing. Coupled with the necessary condition of a skimming incentive based on the calculus of personal gain, the sufficient conditions of asymmetric information and an equity option skimming device, management has a strong incentive to send pirate information signals to the market. Managements have an incentive to contrive corporate information that leads to self-rewarding stock price increases (read the financial history of Global Crossing and JDS Uniphase.). Self-rewarding actions such as mergers and acquisitions and cost consolidations through closures and layoffs are merely deceptive market signals meant to mislead investors into believing that the company is pursuing sustainable growth. These pirate signals (irrational economies) from management distort investor perceptions that lead to investors' "irrational exuberance" and stock price increases. The end results are huge equity option gains for management, earnings restatements, write-offs of the goodwill paid in excess of the value for acquired assets, and sell off of poor-earning assets built up as a result of pirate growth signals.

ZERO-SUM GAME

The stock market is a zero-sum game; someone gains from someone else's loss. Equity options create an environment of competitive game playing by managers for shareholder money. Whether the company is profitable or not, equity option compensation creates a perpetual siphoning off of investors' equity. In the secondary market, they provide management an arbitrage opportunity that is exactly inverse to shareholders' interest.

A market option transaction is a two-sided speculative game where one side gains exactly what the other side loses. Not in an equity option transaction. In an equity option transaction, the corporation forfeits the investors' side of the speculation and allows managers to take risk-free money. Statistically, a risk-free transaction means that there is an absolute certainty of loss to the shareholder. Managers are in an equity call option position and investors are in an equity call writer's position where the loss is exactly the call option seller's gain. Investors are also in a put option position, except that corporations would not provide investors the put options necessary to offset their call losses.

Not only is an equity option a zero-sum game, but a highly weighted transaction (a derivative that provides leverage) where one dollar paid by a manager for an equity option can be cashed out for one hundred, two hundred, or even three hundred dollars or more of an investor's paid-in cost per share. Money comes from the last investors, those who are at-the-money new to the market investors and who may have paid $100 per share. If the stock price declines from $100 to $10 a share, then all those investors who paid $10 or less suffer only paper losses. Not counting transaction costs, all those investors who paid $10.01 or more suffer a real money loss.

Besides being zero sum and leveraged, equity options include the economics of scaled process and parasitic informational advantages. Unlike a bank robbery, where the robber is physically limited by time and space, the microbial process of Internet stock transactions has the viral scaling properties of smallpox. A wealth transfer benefit to management that reallocates investor equity is not only parasitic, but highly infectious to all of corporate society.

SELF-DEALING ZERO-SUM GAME

It is not an overstatement to say that from petty chiseler to world tyrant, the derivative cause of most evil in this world is the power of zero-sum self-dealing. Equity options create a perverse and corrupting incentive to self-dealing. A slot machine is a zero-sum game that will pay the player back once in a while, but someone in a position to exploit the power of a zero-sum game will take all, earn nothing, and give nothing back except maybe an illusory promise.

The games played by management for personal gain against the interest of investors could fill a library. The three most notable games are spinning, flipping, and skimming.

Erik Banks[11] explains how investment bankers and managers, after they have loaded up on equity options, use the tactic of selling a limited number of hot pre IPO stocks. With a shortage of shares available, the price is driven sky-high. Managers then cash out their options at a top price in the secondary market. The number of IPO shares issued is calculated to maximize the stock price in the short run even though the corporation's capitalization suffers from less IPO funding. It is called spinning.

A handmaiden to spinning was once flipping and the rules have now changed to prevent this. This is where managers, employees, and venture capitalists would take their IPO shares and sell them into a hot market as soon as they could after they got them. The law now requires a holding period that bars them from flipping shares. A side note: many companies are being investigated for backdating their equity options at a low market price so they could take advantage of higher stock prices.

Finally, there is the process of equity skimming. Essentially, skimming occurs when the funds taken by managers are not earned. Investors' equity has a liquid quality of flows and pools that makes skimming difficult to measure. Any device that can be used to take an unearned management gain by dipping into these flows or pools is skimming.

The idea that a corporate board made up of golfing buddies who can give each other free cash as bonuses is what skimming is all about. Most legal doctrine on skimming has to do with taking the corporation's capital, but equity options skim money from investors' stock accounts. The corporation is a servant to the process and benefits from its service.

Charles Schwab and his management skimmed nearly a billion dollars from investors in 1999-2002. Fortune12 reported that Mr. Schwab received $353 million while being paid $600 thousand in compensation. What did he do to earn $353 million in three years? He didn't earn it. As chairman of the board, he received this money from the board in the form of equity stock options and gift stock. The rationale that management will align their interests more closely with shareholders by giving them options to own stock does not apply to Mr. Schwab. With Mr. Schwab and his family having 20 percent controlling interest in the Schwab Company, giving him equity stock options and gift stock is not a rational incentive, but a Santa Claus gift from investors.

Charles Schwab's co-CEO, David Pottruck, took a total of $188 million during the same period for a total of $541 million. On average, over twenty-seven thousand investors had to lose at least $20,000 of their investment equity to pay for this rip-off. Beyond equity stock options, Mr. Schwab indulged his sweet tooth for the hourly wage earnings of other people by freeloading on gift stock. As reported in Market Watch. Com (SCH insider, 2006), He received $37,548,980 in gift stock from the Schwab Company—again while collecting salary from the Schwab Company for doing the job he was paid to do. As a member of Sieble System's board, between 1997 and 2004, Mr. Schwab received $61,729,197 in gift stock from Sieble Systems. That comes to $99,287,177 or, as Ms. Smith used to instruct us in the third grade, "We round that up to $100,000,000 in free money." How heartwarming to know that Mr. Schwab thought so much of investors' sweat equity savings, earned on an hourly basis, that he would dip his grateful hands into their pockets and pull out a bonus for himself. All these free gift wealth transfers were supervised under the watchful eyes of the SEC. Did other board members get the same treatment? No! Two questions for the reader. Is this skimming stockholders' money? Is this insider self-dealing? Ask your congressman. How many moms and pops lost most of or all their retirement money to pay for a billionaire's bonus? This was certainly not an investment! Had Schwab not been in business, many people would still have their retirement accounts. If Mr. Schwab wanted diversification or liquidity, he could have sold some of his assets.

Mr. Schwab fired Mr. Pottruck in 2004 for failing, as a CEO, to turn around Schwab Company's stock price. To be fair, there was not much he could do, since management had skimmed most of the Schwab Company's equity support from their most recent shareholders' investments. He and his management merely swept the funds into their accounts. Mr. Charles Schwab was well aware that a turnaround would take time to get new investors back in the market to boost up the stock price again.

The estimate by Fortune is that Mr. Schwab and his management took $951 million of investors' money (on average 47,550 investors had to lose $20,000), and they got away free using a simple device (equity options and gift stock) created by Wall Street and legitimated by Congress. The $951 million figure is only an estimate of investor loss because there is obviously the loss of interest on all that money. Who knows what other shenanigans have been played.

PRIVILEGED KNOWLEDGE

The questions that must be answered are:

1. Did Mr. Schwab have personal knowledge of how equity options would affect the equity value of outsider stockholders?
2. Did he have a personal financial interest in the use of this knowledge?
3. Did he use this knowledge for personal gain at the expense of shareholders?

The unequivocal answer to each of these questions is yes. Mr. Schwab did have personal knowledge of how equity options would affect the equity value of outsider stockholders' shares. Second, he did have a personal financial interest in the use of this knowledge. Third, he did use this knowledge for personal gain at the expense of shareholders.

When market signals to investors are corrupted by management seeking option gains, cheap transaction costs and small dividends merely act as a lure for investors, and have a devastating effect on mom-and-pop shareholding. As a consequence of money being siphoned off through the cash out by management, many mom-and-pop investors are squeezed out of their stock portfolios. How many college tuition funds were lost? How many mortgage payments were missed? How many bankruptcies and divorces resulted from lost stock "investment money"?

Managers who took investors' funds by equity options know better than to expose their gain to the same options that provided their fortunes. They don't reinvest in equity stock option exposures; instead, they seek the safety of government bonds or quality real estate.

Mr. Schwab had a choice that he could have made early in this wealth transfer gambit. He could have sided with his investors who, after all, had made him a multibillionaire, or he could have taken sides against them in favor of his own self-interests and the interests of his management friends. He didn't see any reason to side with the faceless names on computer files whose earned savings made him rich when he could instead side with his lunch buddies who were sure to think of him as a big shot for helping them rip off investors too.

Could he be excused for not seeing that the long-term interest of his namesake company lay in the long-term savings of these faceless investors? Or did he really believe that the stock market, as now practiced, is nothing more than a Ponzi scheme where he takes the money off the top and new investors pay off the losses of earlier investors?

There was no market determination for management's gain because it was strictly based on insider decision making. Just as Congress has, at times, made graft honest for themselves, they have made skimming shareholder wealth honest for corporate management. Where is the protection against conflict of interest in an arm's-length transaction when the corporation's board of directors and management are gifting free money to themselves from the shareholders' equity pool?

The only way investors will be able to recoup skimmed losses is to wait for new investors' money. Look up the definition of a Ponzi. Was Mr. Charles Schwab a gatekeeper of investors' savings? Is this what Adam Smith meant by the "invisible hand"?

ASYMMETRIC INFORMATION

Like a river, information has an upstream and a downstream. Upstream information from management insiders is both temporally and spatially asymmetric to downstream investors. Upstream water pollution is almost impossible for those downstream to detect without expert evaluation. It is only after the damage has been done that the right questions can be formulated, but by then it is too late to save what is lost. Like Schwab, Enron, and others, pollution effects of deceptive information from management financial reporting are impossible to evaluate without expert knowledge; by the time it has been evaluated, it's too late to recover what is lost.

A measure of how asymmetric information impacted the stock market in 2000–2001 is evidenced by the enormity of wealth transfer.

David Zion explains the cash flow consequences of equity stock options:

In our view, the actual transfer of wealth takes place from shareholders to employees when the options are exercised....We thus tried to measure this transfer of wealth for the companies in the S&P 500....It was at its peak in 2000 with a $117.9 billion transfer of wealth, about 18 percent of cash flow from operations. 13

Zion makes a distinction between the company and the shareholders. He explains that these funds do not come from corporate cash; but come from the equity principal of shareholders. Zion makes the point that in 2000, Applied Micro Circuits was granting options to employees with a fair market value of $1 million per employee. He says, "One has to wonder whether some companies were paying any attention to the cost of their employee stock option plans."14 Question: what did the mailroom clerk do to earned a million-dollar bonus? How about the janitor? Could Mom and Pop afford this bonus from their savings?

Investors receive their compensation information indirectly from management. Management does all the accounting for their gains and investors' losses. Those who got away with the money hold the only explanation for such huge investor losses. It's like the police robbing your house and then accounting for the robbery. Investors were disadvantaged by asymmetry15 of relevant and timely information. The public's losses to management were a direct result of management's calculated lack of credibility.

The SEC's response to what has been described by Erik Banks as "$6 trillion of market value sucked out of investors' pockets from 2000 to 2003"16 was to ask insiders for more disclosure— a lame and ineffective response. The SEC allowed a fashionable financial device that materially changed the rules of ownership to be used in the public market without a thorough vetting or assessment of its harmful consequences to investors.

Luisa Beltran,17 reported that ten Wall Street firms paid $1.4 billion to settle charges of deceiving investors with biased stock research. Why take such damaging risks to their reputations and integrity? One reason is that, as management insiders, they were selling equity-optioned stock that they held for their own accounts. Oil company managers are cashing in millions of dollars in equity options as bonuses for their companies' stock price increases. Is there a perverse short-term incentive at work here to raise the price of gas?

Mark Twain said, "A lie can go halfway around the world before the truth even gets its boots on." It is no aggregation that when you hitch a lie to a truth, you can confound people's reasoning about an issue for many years—Mussolini, Stalin…Insiders will always be one step ahead in the self-dealing use of information they disclose to the investing public.

BOARDS OF DIRECTORS

Outside investors are effectively third parties to a company's decision making on compensation policy. Investors must depend on the honesty, integrity, and diligence of the board to protect their interest. However, corporate boards have about as much common interest in minority shareholders as did feudal kings in their subjects' interests. Kings and boards have found that without a market's influence, what serves their own interest directs what they think serves the interests of those they are supposed to serve. It was the duty of a feudal king to watch over the interests of his subjects, but that duty was translated into what the king considered their interests to be after all of his self-dealing. Likewise, it is the duty of the board to watch over the interests of shareholders, but those interests too are translated into what the board thinks are investor interests after it has skimmed investor money.

Boards have failed miserably to protect investors' interests. Colin B. Carter and Jay W. Lorsch explain, "Management and boards, loaded up with stock and options, are subject to a powerful conflict of interest....Attempts to achieve...alignment in some companies have thus led to directors' interest being aligned with management rather than with shareholders."18 Carter and Lorsch have confirmed a truism for most corporate boards.

PROXY DISCLOSURE

A critical flaw of corporate proxy disclosures is that they do not tell the investing public how the process of equity stock options work. Without this information, investors have been completely misled about their investments. For most investors, the idea of a corporation's compensation responsibility suggests that the company goes out into the market and buys stocks for its executives out of company money. It would make sense for a company to deduct the cost of buying stocks for its employees as a company expense. The "options" would merely reflect the amount of stock bought by the company for its executives.

What is not disclosed is that companies pay nothing for equity stock options; they don't disclose that these options are wealth transfers from shareholders to the company's managers. Proxy disclosures are mostly ambiguous half-truths and omissions. Even if, however, the wealth transfer were made as clear as glass, they would still be a fraud on investors for the reasons given in this paper.

A QUESTION OF LEGITIMACY

Questioning the legitimacy of corporate wealth transfers is important. Just because Congress has legislated a legal status for the use of equity options does not mean that legality of their use will stand up to constitutional scrutiny. The question of legitimacy arises from a threefold consideration: the legitimate use of investor stock equity investment for a compensation expense in the secondary stock market, self-dealing collusion of boards and managers, and the role of the corporation in transferring investors' ownership to corporate management.

What purpose is served for investors to own stock if they have no individual protection from management predations? Investors expose their savings to ownership risks from a corporate investment while management is allowed to swap that ownership stake for promises they cannot keep. Earned savings swapped for empty promises merely gives management insiders, who are already getting paid to do their best, incentive to deceive. No market determination is made for management wealth transfers; their gain is strictly based on insider decision making.

This subverts the purpose of investing in stock. Collusion between boards and management to transfer investor wealth for their personal gain violates, if not the law, the spirit of management's fiduciary duty of loyalty and care to shareholders. Management receives compensation as an obligation of the company for employment, and the employment is an obligation of management to make a good faith best effort to serve shareholders' interest. Compensation and bonuses, as an employment cost to the company, are supposed to be a measured and affordable expense of a company. Any evasion by management to do their best for the corporation and the interest of shareholders is a material breach of their obligation and reason for termination. By shifting the cost of compensation from the corporation to shareholders through equity stock, the corporation breaches its obligation to serve shareholders' interests.

THE PERIL OF EQUITY WEALTH TRANSFERS

A significant peril of equity wealth transfers comes from the macro-level dynamics of cost shifting that are not factored into the compensation decisions boards make on the micro-finance level. What logic justifies shifting corporate compensation costs to the equity savings of retirements? If corporations cannot afford these compensation costs, how can one suppose that such affordability could be supported by investors' savings accounts? Two market dynamics of equity option cost shifting suggest that the retirements of many in America are in peril.

First, huge amounts of stock market money have been aggregated by managed funds, mutual funds, etc. . ., and large wealth transfers are being accomplished by the leveraging power of options. This means that individual investor decisions are not effectively directing the market bidding process for stocks. The small transaction investor who would provide immediate feedback of gain or loss does not populate the market. Losers don't drop out of the market; they are a part of a bigger pool that is shrinking. Winners are commingled with losers.

It is all in the zeros. Published in 1998, The Vanguard Guide To Planning For Retirement19 estimated there were nearly seven thousand mutual funds in the United States with a total $3.5 trillion equity invested. Reducing these numbers down to an analogous comparison will uncover the hidden perils of option-related wealth transfers. First, see that there are twelve zeros in a trillion and nine zeros in a billion. Now, let's subtract from the $3.5 trillion the amount of $100 billion. That leaves $3.4 trillion. Wow, this has no sense of reality.

Let's look at it another way. Suppose you owned a gas storage tank that contained thirty-five hundred gallons of gas. If a thief came along and siphoned off one hundred gallons, would you miss them? Not unless you had a very precise measuring system and you were careful to measure your tank's total gallons every day. Now, to confound your problem, if suppliers were adding and subtracting gas from the tank every day, it would become almost impossible to detect how much they siphoned. The ratio of thirty-five hundred gallons of gas to one hundred gallons siphoned is the same as $3.5 trillion to $100 billion in stockholders' equity. There is an opportunity to siphon a lot of retirement money out of savers' pockets before it will be detected. With $200 billion in funds, if a state retirement fund loses $10 billion (ten gallons from a two-hundred-gallon tank) it reacts by looking for ways to recoup its losses. It goes after more risk to leverage more return. If it fails to regain what it lost, it either distributes a smaller pie to the investors or it appeals to the government to subsidize its losses.

Second, options provide leverage that can pull huge sums of money out of a retirement fund's equity position, and there is little or no feedback to the market. Wealth transfers in large funds are almost invisible. Currently, there is little regulatory responsibility for oversight. The leverage effect of options is a very slippery concept to grasp. Another metaphorical example will help convey what is meant by option leverage. Without getting caught up in the mechanics of leverage, it is possible for a person with the use of ropes and pulley to lift an elephant. The mechanics are such that pulleys can provide enough leverage for a person to overcome the gravitational weight of the elephant.

Options have this same kind of leverage effect on stocks. A very small amount of money can be used to cash out a very large amount of expensive stocks. The net result is a large stealthy wealth transfer from many stockholders to one or two corporate executives.

INVESTOR ALIGNMENT

Investors spend much of their life laboring and sacrificing short-term consumption to save for retirement. The Federal Reserve estimates that on average 3 percent of income is saved annually. In arithmetic terms, for $20,000 to be saved, there has to be $20,000/.03 = $666,666$ in gross salary earned. Of course, many have benefited from other investments and inflation to supplement their retirement fund. But it is not easy to save for a satisfactory retirement. At a 3 percent savings rate, the earnings needed to save $951 million—$951 million$/.03=$3.17$ trillion in gross wages. Investors will have to work for $3.17 trillion in earnings to recover their lost savings. Standard & Poor's 500 Guide, 2003 edition, reports that the Schwab Company's clients' assets declined from $872 billion in 2000 to $846 billion in 2001 for a total drop of $26 billion. Only the managers at Schwab know how much of this was due to wealth transfer. This is just from the Schwab Company.

The justification for owning a stock is to get the highest return possible given the risk involved. Investors are not motivated by charity or social experimentation, but by return of their principal and return on their principal. Most investors do not consciously buy rat holes or blue-sky pie. If investors are made aware that their stocks are loaded with embedded options; they will not knowingly expose their saving to such a wealth transfer. When they understand the consequences of buying a stock with embedded options, they intuitively know that it is worse than buying swampland. At least with swampland they own the value of the snakes. They recognize that a wealth transfer is a lot like putting money into a slot machine that is out of order.

PROFIT

Profit is one goal that aligns the interests of management, the corporation, and shareholders. Profit represents a return that investors, managers, and the corporation can all share without cost shifting or equity skimming. Profits provide compensation without disconnecting this alignment. The corporation is well served by being allowed to employ management supported by measurable compensation costs that lead to an honest bottom line. Society and the economy benefit when managers do not get access to huge amounts of investor money. Corporations and managers should not get rich at the expense of an investor's reduced equity position. Equity options fail to do what they were supposed to do—align the interest of the corporation, managers, and shareholders. Assuming shareholders are paid for their risks, profit sharing is a way to bring about such an alignment. Profits have an earned and distributive quality that equates input with output while equity compensation has an unearned and redistributive quality that equates gain with conflict of interests in the use of discretionary power and self-dealing.

Equity compensation is a self-destructive device that ends when stockholders are no longer able or willing to expose their savings to theft by management. The problem, as always, is the next new scheme by management to breach established boundaries.

REGULATION, LAW, AND COMPETITION

Regulation of the stock market has proven to be ineffective. One way to defeat parasitic self-dealing is not through regulation, but by laws forbidding it. The problem here is defining the scope of all possible breaches in a law leaving no holes and preventing compromises created by a self-interested Congress. Ownership rights legislation is probably the one best way to provide a comprehensive solution.

Another way, which doesn't rely on the honesty of Congress, is to create a business that competes head-to-head with the likes of Charles Schwab and differentiates itself by the way it builds and maintains investors' trust.

This type of business would set the standard that all other competitors would have to follow in order to compete. The standard would by charter forbid all wealth transfers of investors' equity and forbid all discretionary board decision making that involved owners' equity. Investors would have rights that set and kept their interest above the decision-making powers of the board. The result would be to drive self-dealers out of the market. The memory of Mr. Schwab and his company would be just a memory.

SUMMARY

Equity options disconnect the investor from the investment and the company's management from their duty to protect the interest of shareholders. It is a contradiction to invest in something that cannot be owned. It is illusory for investors to buy some vague future promise to do some vague future something that has already been contracted and paid for by a corporate employer through salaried compensation. The value of an equity stock option to management is inversely related to the value of an investor's ownership account. Like a risk-free bank robbery, equity options may be an incentive to management, but they are a deadweight loss to small-money investors. The recent scandals involving backdating of options is analogous to a bank robber rescheduling the timing of his robbery to coincide with how much is in the vault.

Why is it so difficult to uncover the fatal flaws inherent in an equity option? One reason is that the process is not monopolistic economic predation, but parasitic financial predation. Success is achieved by device and stealth of information asymmetries rather than by economic control. Vague laws that are supposed to protect shareholders have proven to be ineffectual and costly. When an investor has suffered a loss at the hands of an unscrupulous stock dealer or corporation a la Enron, and Global Crossing, the only recourse has been to seek damages through the courts, but that is impossible for small-money investors who have already lost their savings. Regulation by disclosure is regulation by information. However, asymmetric information entirely contaminates the value of disclosure as a valid market regulator. Regulation by disclosure will never overcome the corrupting power of insiders' informational advantage.

The flaws in equity compensation cannot be overcome. The money taken via equity compensation in any form as a wealth transfer is a deceptive and fraudulent shift of a corporation's compensation expense to a minority of most recent investors. Equity compensation taken out of a shareholder's ownership account is not an investment. It is an expense that creates no value for the most recent investor either as return of investment or return on investment. The corporation may benefit by paying an equity bonus, but it is at the cost of skimming investors' ownership interest.

A perpetual fraud: The stock market is seed, root, and branch a fraud on investors. The current situation is the result of years of Wall Street lobbying Congress for self-serving legislation resulting in a poison tree that bears poison fruit. Mom-and-pop earners from Main Street invest money in stocks, and then management insiders from Wall Street—stockbrokers like Charles Schwab, and top corporate managers—cash money out of the investor equity. As long as Mom and Pop keep adding to mutual funds and pension funds, management insiders will keep milking these 401(k) funds, state/county pension funds, and hollowing out individual mom-and-pop investors' equity money. Some state retirement funds are doing better than others are simply because Wall Street firm managers have been supervising the operations.

The entire predatory subprime housing losses, credit declines, corporate write-downs, and stock market losses such as Fannie Mae and Freddie Mac losses and Bear Stearns losses are tied to the perverse incentives for skimming hundreds of billions of dollars taken out of the market as compensation by Wall Street insiders.

Wall Street executives such as Treasury Secretary Henry Paulson skimmed hundreds of millions out of Goldman Sachs' stocks investors' money. Sandy Weill skimmed millions from Citigroup shareholders, and JP Morgan Chase, Merrill Lynch, Morgan Stanley, Lehman Brothers, Bear Stearns, Charles Schwab, and E-Trade are just a few of the financial companies where management insiders took hundreds of millions out of shareholders' money. The technology and pharmaceutical industries are crowded with the same skimming activities.

All that they teach at the university about finance is dependent upon the trust of those who use the decision-making information of financial theory for purposes intended. The stock market works only if investors can trust those who use their information honestly, and do not use it for deceptive or manipulative self-dealing ends.

FOUR RECOMMENDATIONS

(I) Deception and manipulation contaminate all of this wealth transfer money, and Congress should force the return of these savings back to those who were cheated. A reparation committee should conduct an investigation into who will refund how much to whom, and determine legislation needed to carry out its recommendations. Unfortunately, since many currently in Congress have benefited directly or indirectly from gifts by those who were doing the cheating, this recommendation is not likely to be carried out by them.

(2) Conduct a congressional investigation into how and why shareholders were made so vulnerable to the transfer of their wealth into the hands of plundering managements using an equity option device. Apropos of this investigation, Congress should outlaw all forms of equity compensation. The market, not the corrupting influence of a few individuals, should arbitrate equity values. As well, the Congress should finally enact into law clear shareholders' ownership rights that cannot be manipulated by corporate boards or managers.

(3) As difficult as it would be for Congress to investigate itself, leaders in Congress, uncompromised by Wall Street money and power, should conduct an investigation into the influence of Wall Street on Congress. Attorneys, qualified by their independence of Wall Street connections and influence, should take a leading role in the examination of witnesses.

(4) This report has uncovered just the tip of a huge iceberg of self-dealing. It is recommended that Congress investigate Schwab's mutual fund activities to find out if stocks were being traded to maximize his equity option wealth transfers.

ENDNOTES

[1] In the case of self-dealing with equity options, there are, of course, intentional and unintentional participation. Some managers, as terms of employment, are forced to accept options. They are not the target of this paper. The difference between parasitic gain and a financial parasite is defined by intention and control. A manager or employee forced to take parasitic gain at the risk of losing his or her job is a collateral victim. A financial parasite feeds off its host and benefits from the harm it does. The only consequence to a host from the actions of a parasite is degeneration. It is like eating a sandwich and then having the sandwich eat you.

[2] Self-dealing is defined as taking one's own financial gains at the expense of someone else through whatever means possible. This definition implies a process of parasitic wealth transfer where there has not been an exchange of value for value, such as in this case between management and shareholders. Insider self-dealing by Wall Street was the single most important cause of the 1929 depression.

[3] Winnick is a professional sleaze who paid heavily for Washington lobbyists, lawyers, and political "buy-in" to straighten out any crooked angles in his financial manipulations. He gave millions to his Synagogue, but then Hitler gave to his charities too. See Julie Creswell and Nomi Prin, "The Emperor of Greed," Fortune, June 24, 2002, 6; Mark Gimein, "You Bought, They Sold," Fortune, September 2, 2002, p. 64; Robert H. Tillman and Michael L. Indergaard, Pump and Dump; The Rancid Rules of the New

Economy (New Brunswick: Rutgers University Press, 2005), 115-120.

[4] You will note that the word profit is never used to describe the gains taken through a wealth transfer; profits are an earned residual of a value-for-value transaction that is not the result of self-dealing manipulations.

[5] Charles Fishman, "You Can Quote Him," Fast Company, July 2001, FC48.

[6] Two books are essential reading: (1) Ferdinand Pecora, Wall Street Under Oath (Clifton N.J.: Augustus M. Kelley Publishers, 1973), republished from the original Simon & Schuster, 1939. (2) Adolf Berle and Gardiner Means, The Modern Corporation and Private Property, revised edition (New York: Harcourt, Brace & World, 1968. Though I disagree with Joel Seligman's statement about Pecora on p. 2 of his book, it is an excellent account of how Wall Street ripped off the public. Joel Seligman, The Transformation of Wall Street (Boston: Northwestern University Press, 1995).

[7] Jack Davis. "Webb Has Sold $90 Million Since Joining Company," San Jose Mercury News, 24 July 2006, sec E, P. 2E.

[8] Equity stock options are leveraged claims against the money of an investor's stock account. They are wealth transfers from investor to manager. There is no capital from the corporation used for this transfer of wealth to management.

[9] A zero sum game results in one person's gain from another person's loss, as opposed to a positive sum game where both participants gain from a value-for-value exchange.

[10] If you pay $35 for a stock, you are at-the-money, if the stock price goes down to $12; you are out-of-the- money by $23.

[11] An equity option is a derivative transfer device. It derives its transfer value from the underlying stock. It gives the holder the

right, but not the obligation to buy a stock at a predetermined price, called the strike price. The compensation committee of the board of directors determines the number of options to be issued and the strike price.

[12].Erik Banks, The Failure of Wall Street—How and Why Wall Street Fails And What Can Be Done About It (New York: Palgrave Macmillan, 2004), 130-131.

[13] Mark Gimein, "The Greedy Bunch: You Bought, They Sold," Fortune, Sept. 2, 2002.

[14] David Zion, CFA, "The Cost of Employee Stock Options," in Analyzing, Researching, and Valuing Equity Investments, CFA Institute Conference Proceeding, 1—2 December 2004, Philadelphia, ed. Rodney N. Sullivan, CFA (Charlottesville, Virginia, CFA Institute Conference Proceedings, 21 June 2005) 54.

[15] Ibid., 53.

[16] When a seller has knowledge of defects in a market transaction not known to the buyer, and takes financial advantage of the buyer's ignorance, the seller has an asymmetric informational advantage over the buyer.

[17] Erik Banks, The Failure of Wall Street, 98.

[18] Lisa Beltran, CBS. MarketWatch.com, Dec 20, 2002, www.marketwatch.com/News/Story...5/18/2006, Matt Andrejczak contributed to the story.

[19] Colin B. Carter and Jay W. Lorsch, Back to the Drawing Board—Designing Corporate Boards For A Complex World (Boston: Harvard Business School Press, 2004), 48.

[20] The Vanguard Group, The Vanguard Guide To Planning For Retirement, 3rd ed., (New York: McGraw-Hill, 1998), 63.

THE SELF-DEALING INSIDER
BY
MICHAEL R. LA CRONE (MAY 2006)

Man buys to build, upon his land;
Soon finds his castle, sunk in sand!
Investor too; stocks, she planned;
Takes her loss, at the broker's hand!
Contrived deception, purpose subverted;
Empty promises, carefully worded!
Financial ruin, investments a waste;
Equity stolen; pensions debased!
Foul is the deed, what is the aim?
Self-dealing greed! A zero-sum game!
Parasite on labor, insider by name;
Predators' sport; the victim to blame!
Politician the servant, regulation, and rule;
Duplicitous dealer, the insider's tool!
What's to be done? A critical flaw;
Ownership rights? The rule of law?
Illusory claims; a ballot, no sense;
An equity bullet, the last defense!
Justice awry, that allows such a cost;
Justice restored, that returns all was lost!
Copyright ©

ADDITIONAL THOUGHTS:

WASHINGTON'S BAILOUT OF WALL STREET: A RIP-OFF FOR INVESTORS AS WELL AS TAXPAYERS
By
Dr. Michael R. La Crone (DBA '96-Finance)
12-18-2008

Most insiders on Wall Street would like to turn the page on the current recession so that they could get back to business. The business they would get back to would be doing what they were doing. Namely, using the same old devices and deceptions they used to help create our current financial problems.

What Congress did with the $700 billion bailout money merely buried the financial frauds of Wall Street under a mountain of cash. What Congress didn't do was get to the bottom of Wall Street's misbehavior and take the guilty to task for their financial felonies. Instead, the guilty were given bailout money to re-capitalize the investment banks that these insiders bankrupted. In addition to the money ripped-off from the stock market; our tax dollars are now paying these same Wall Street insiders to employ Washington lobbyists and financially support members of Congress through campaign contributions.

What did not change was the opportunity to use the same old devices and deceptions to continue their "stock price skimming" of new investors' money. When the CEO of Goldman Sachs, Lloyd Blankfein, declared that he would take a dollar a year in compensation, he omitted to mention that he had already free loaded over a million gift stocks and award of stocks. The bailout money will re-inflate Goldman Sachs stock price, so the amount of money coming from these shares would, no doubt, bring in substantially more money than corporate compensation. All at Shareholders' expense!

The critical element missing in all of the Congressional investigatory activity of Wall Street has been to ask "where did all the money go that caused a need for the bailout?" Treasury Secretary Hank Paulson knows "Who got da money." He got over $200 million of da money while he was the CEO for Goldman Sachs. Executives of these Wall Street firms are loaded up with millions of freeloaded shares.

What is stock price skimming? As I explain in my book, The Charles Schwab Stock Rip Off, stock price skimming occurs when an at-the-money (explained below) investor buys $10,000 worth of stock, and within a fraction of a second a manager, Charles Schwab, Henry Paulson, Lloyd Blankfein cashes out $5 or $6 million dollars of their gift stock. When insiders cash out their free shares, they reduce the total value of the stock outstanding by the amount they took out of the market. If there are many new buyers in the market, the loss will be offset and the price will not go down, but as more free shares are cashed out, less new money will be available to maintain the shares' price and the effects of price skimming will drive the stocks' price down. Let's say that you buy a stock online for $100, this means you are at-the-money for $100. If the stock price declines by $10, you are out-of-the-money by $10. (Dilution of earnings is not directly relevant to stock price skimming.) The only way that the at-the-money investor can get her money back is through new investors. Stock options and gift stock represent a ponzi fraud embedded in the stock purchased by at-the- money investors.

Essentially, insiders are competing with new investors for new investors' money without putting up any money. There is no risk for insiders and no return for investors. This strategy selectively skims new at-the-money investors' funds and does not affect those investors who are deep-in-the-money (bought stock at a lower price). Over time, at-the-money investors are squeezed out of the stock because total new investors' money has not grown fast enough to offset what has been siphoned off the market. Mr. Schwab has ripped off more than a billion dollars of at-the-money investors funds and, so far, gotten away with it. Oracle CEO Larry Ellison has cashed millions of gift shares. This is money that is not reinvested in the market.

From investment banks such as Goldman Sachs and J. P. Morgan, to Commercial banks, Bank of America, Wells Fargo, to technology companies, Cisco, Intel, Oracle, to blue chip companies, IBM, Proctor and Gamble, Dell, to oil companies, Exxon, Conoco Phillips, to pharmaceuticals, Pfizer, Merck, the list goes on and on; self dealing management insiders have received millions of free shares that they are cashing out for hundreds of billions of dollars in shareholders' money. Again, this money does not return to the stock market. The companies that gave insider managers these free shares did not pay a cent for them and, besides a tax deduction, get no money for them.

New at-the-money investors do not want to put their savings in to a stock for an opportunity to get their money skimmed by insiders, but Congress has not disclosed this pig-in-the-poke, and that's the way self- dealing insiders on Wall Street like it. What these managers are taking from shareholders is unearned and parasitic. Stock price skimming of shareholders' equity is a vicious fraud on unsuspecting investors brought about by Wall Street's corrupt influence on Washington. Investors lost savings that took many years to save and it will take many years of savings to restore all the purchasing power lost. Young people have 30 years of work ahead of them to recover, but older people will never recover. No government bailout will restore the earned savings stolen by this egregious insider freeloading. Insiders took their gains by committing fraud on investors. If government wants to restore this economy then it needs to require that management insiders return, from their insider accounts, the hundreds of billions of dollars in shareholders' money.

THE WASHINGTON BAILOUT OF WALL STREET CRIMINALS
By
Dr. Michael R. La Crone 7/11/2009

It is important to recognize that banks do not make loan decisions. Bank managers make loan decisions. And, bank managers do not make dumb loans. Highly skilled and conservative bank managers make bad loans, loans that cannot possibly be repaid, but they do not make dumb loans. Top executives who receive gift stock bonus compensation at Goldman Sachs, Bank of America, Citigroup, Bear Sterns, Lehman, Wells Fargo Merrill Lynch, J.P. Morgan, and Morgan Stanley had full knowledge their bad loans could not and would not be repaid. The investment bank loans, subprime and otherwise, that have been defaulting were fully understood by the investment bankers who provided the money to loan. They knew the debt capacity of thinly capitalized borrowers. They were well aware that loan defaults were going to happen, and they were prepared to make excuses and blame their employees, lack of regulation, borrowers, etc...for the crises.

What would compel a rational banker to lend money on loans that could not be repaid? There is a very rational answer. Banker's bonus payments are made in gift stocks and stock options. When the bank's stock price goes up then bankers' bonus income goes up. Attempting to boost a company's stock price is called stock price maximization. A rational banker has a very personal reason to make bad loans, because in the short-term, bad loans translate into improved revenues. Increased revenues are a market signal to buy stocks. Buying stocks raises the stock price, and managers cash them out. A stock bonus plan based on long-term company performance is still a fraud on investors. The money that comes from value investors (low cost stock) and growth investors (high cost stock) are both being skimmed and can only be recovered from the money of new investors.

Here is the fraud. The money that managers get from cashing out their gift and optioned stocks comes from stock investors. Every dollar taken out of the stock market in bonus compensation reduces the value of that stock by a dollar. The only way that the stock price can be improved is through new stock investors. The lie used to rationalize and legitimize bonus gift and optioned stock is that these gifts help align the interest of managers with shareholders. There is no possible way that managers can align their interest with shareholders through bonus stock. There is an inverse (opposing) relationship between managers' bonus wealth and shareholders' wealth where managers are competing for shareholders' money with shareholders' money. To reduce the many gift stocks dumped on the market, management merely buys back the stock using corporate earnings. Earnings used to buy back stocks could be used to pay dividends, fund employee health care, and finance employee retirements. According to Warren Buffett, the stock market crash of 2002 was the biggest wealth transfer in the history of America.

Washington's political leaders put on a lot of public relations rhetoric and theater to pacify public outrage, but these politicians know the public's memory is short. Wall Street's lobby money will go a long way to maintain legitimacy of the status quo. What consequences are there for the bankers and the banks from making bad loans? The bank's shareholders and bond holders incur devastating losses of equity capital and loan capital, but corporate bank managers face no financial consequences except the loss of their jobs and maybe diminished reputational capital. Given the huge bonus checks that will fund their progeny for centuries, these small trade-offs are very rational.

Wall Street's gift stock compensation model has spread like a virus to corporations' management across America and the globe. This does not diminish the fraud that it is or the lies on which it is based. Wide use of Wall Street's corrupt compensation model helps to defuse the public's outrage. Joseph Stalin said One death is a tragedy; one million is a statistic! In the same sense, if a lie is used by a few, it's an outrage, if a lie is used by many, it's too big to question. Wall Street managers are using a page out of Hitler's propaganda book. Hitler said, Make the lie big, make it simple, keep saying it, and eventually they will believe it!

Bankers have another reason to make bad loans that could bankrupt their banks. The Banks were "too big to fail' as some pundits cautioned. Wall Street investment bankers have an incentive to make bad loans because they are assured that the federal government will bail them out after their loans go bad. The federal government set precedence by bailing out the Savings and Loan industry in the 1980s. Henry Paulson, as former CEO of Goldman Sachs, not only took $200 million in stock bonus compensation, but as Treasury secretary to former president George W. Bush, he initiated the Wall Street bailout that saved the bonus money of Goldman Sachs management. A sweet deal! Tax payers recapitalized the banks that recapitalized the bank's stock that recapitalized management's bonus money.

The arrogance of these Wall Street executives was noted in a Bloomberg article by Peter S. Green, Merrill's Thane Said to Pay $1.2 million to Decorator. According to Green, Merrill Lynch

CEO John Thane spent $87,000 for a rug and $25,000 for a pedestal table while he was in the process of firing employees. Not only were bankers immune to the consequences of making bad loans, they could become the heroes who saved the banks from future devastating losses. Time for more bonus money!

What will these willful bankers do next? You can bet it will involve more self-dealing gains at the cost to investors, bond holders, and tax payers. Washington's elite will continue to side with the money of Wall Street over the losses of Main Street. Beyond their subprime crimes, these bankers stole widows and orphans' milk money, and mom and pops' rocking chair money. They did more damage to people's lives than Bernard Madoff, and deserve the same amount of time that Madoff received. As decision making insiders, investment bankers' and stock brokers' use of financial device and deceit for illegitimate gain is predatory and parasitic. These bankers are not too big to jail!

- Historically; in another time, these financial predators would have been hanged for looting the wealth of their neighbors.
- Idealistically; real justice would have the president of the United States declare martial law. Marshals would take Wall Street executives and those in Congress who helped them to face a court. The court would strip them of their wealth and send them to prison.
- Realistically; Congress should form and empower an investigative agency that could force the return of all the wealth looted from investors' to be repaid with interest. This would set a new standard of behavior for Wall Street and Congress.

OBAMA AND WALL STREET
By
Dr. Michael La Crone
3/20/2009

Recently, president Obama was quoted in the Bloomberg news (Bloomberg March 3 2009) as saying that it may be a good time for long term investors to put their money in the stock market. Unlike the duplicity and deceit of our recent failure Mr. Bush, I believe that president Obama has a sincere heart, and would not intentionally mislead the public. However, he is being misled by the very bankers who contrived this current financial betrayal.

Mr. Obama is, it seems, absolutely clueless when it comes to recognizing the potential disaster for the mom and pop who might follow through on his remarks and expose their savings to a rigged stock market. It looks as if Wall Street insiders have persuaded Mr. Obama to believe that getting Bush out of the White House is all that was needed to clean up Washington. There has been no change in the conditions or change of the insiders who created the condition that have led to this economic disaster. The same Wall Street insiders are now getting bailout money for their criminal frauds on the public. The same corporate boards are still writing themselves checks in the form of gift stocks on shareholders' accounts.

Obama, appointing as arbiters of the bank bailout policy, those Wall Street insiders who either helped to corrupt the banks or who, by omission, allowed the banks to be corrupted is an act of political naiveté or worse. Bush's Treasury Secretary Henry

Paulson (Goldman Sachs) took over $200 million, Mary Schapiro served as Chairman and CEO of the NASD, as Chairman of the Commodity Futures Trading Commission and as a Commissioner on the Securities and Exchange Commission was on the boards of Duke Energy and Kraft Foods taking gift shares, Timothy Geithner served as president and CEO of the Federal Reserve Bank of New York. He was responsible for oversight of Wall Street's business practices.

Many members of Congress are in the pockets of these Wall Street swindlers and so Congress has done nothing to bring these criminals to justice. Congressional enquiry always point to the financial problems facing banks and how badly they need to be bailed out. All the huff and puff theater provided by the congressional hearing on what happened to the banks never gets around to asking who did it, how they did it, why they did it, how much they got for doing it, when will they pay restitution to compensate investors for losses? How much will they pay in punitive damages? How much time will they serve in prison? Congressional leaders with the help of government appointed Wall Street insiders have provided Wall Street investment banks tax payer funds to wash all the deceitful transactions out of their balance sheets. Ex-President Bush and some in Congress should face the same questions.

From the beginning, Wall Street's history is littered with larcenous behavior that has led to the financial ruin of trusting investors. This current economic upheaval is not the first time that mom and pop investors have been wiped out by Wall Street and Washington. There has been a traitorous (parasitic quid pro quo) relationship between insiders from both Wall Street and Washington towards the publics' interest since Wall Street's beginning. Congress has relied upon the short memory and naïveté of a remote constituency to devise legislation that undermined the publics' financial stability and trust. Wall Street continuously engineers the deceptions and devices needed to rip off shareholders' invested savings.

The current economic crisis was caused by the failure of bank management insiders that caused the failure of banks. Using tax payer money to recapitalize failed banks is the recapitalization of the managers who caused the banks to fail. Corporate managers pursued short term revenues from any source available as a way to justify stock compensation. These managers gave themselves gift stock compensation (tantamount to counterfeit money) that drained off real money from 401(K) pension funds, mom and pop investment funds and government retirement funds. They merely sweep the money from cashing out free stock into their bonus accounts.

Stockholders' equity provided huge amounts of money that no corporations could ever afford. Corporate boards made up their stock awards out of thin air. Awards that cost the corporation nothing! The money corporate managers received from cashing out gift shares paid for by shareholders' equity were as criminal as if a gun was used in a robbery. Earned savings were transferred form those who worked for the money to managers who used deceit as their weapon. In the sense that a bank robbery was committed, corporate insiders didn't just steal retirement money; they stole your rights of ownership to your earned investment money. That is slavery economics.

I have a set of data showing that (10) executives out of five companies were given over 200,000,000 gift shares by their corporate boards. This number does not include the other executives of these companies whose gift shares I did not count. Multiply $100 a share times $200 million. That is the kind of money being skimmed by management insiders. Stocks are as liquid and valuable as cash. When corporate Insiders can give themselves and top managers millions of free shares, they are counterfeiting an illegitimate claim on real money.

We have to ask; when will the publics' regulatory servants quit acting as an agent for corrupt insiders? When will the pretense of representative government stop? When will we get justice from Wall Street's offending investment charade? When will a court finally investigate congressional behavior for criminal conspiracies? When will the public demand that courts impose responsibility for the frauds committed by insiders who make Wall Street's decisions?

SCRIPTING CONGRESS
By
Dr. Michael La Crone
8-19-2009

In the middle Ages, when a corrupt Roman church domi-
nated Europe, people would protest against the rules governing
the church. Church leaders would tell them," we can do nothing
to change the rules; we are followers bound by rules given to us by
God". How did God create rules for the church? God's rules for
the church were written by his followers. The moral here is: Those
who write the script determine the rules for what is right and what
is wrong; the script governs those who get what and those who pay
what, those who are benefited and those who are burdened, those
who are Beneficiaries and those who are benefactors. In government, the script writer's liberty is legitimacy by the script, for all
others, the script is law.

*Self-serving implies that a person is in a position of power. That power
provides opportunities for a person to improve their personal wealth through the
use of that power.*

*Self-dealing implies that a person is in a position of power. That person uses
their power to transfer unearned wealth into their own account from the earned
wealth of others.*

A question on the minds of many people is: how is it that
so much time and tax payer money has been expended by Congress investigating Wall Street financial crises? Crises that have
continued to occur over and over since 1929, and yet Congress
has not found a lasting solution? Each financial crisis brings about

new regulations, and then comes a new financial crisis that creates losses for investors greater than the previous one. The answer is found when you look at the money to be made by Wall Street power brokers through their ability to craft self-serving congressional legislation. Wall Street has developed connections with Congress that provide new opportunities to deceive the public through manipulation of loop-holes and gaps in law for their own financial self-dealing gains.

Congress, the Senate and House of Representatives, is a collection of individuals representing the voters of their districts and states. Many of them are lawyers. As representatives, they are confronted with a long line of special pleaders, special interest groups, who want the tax payer to fund their private interest. They are, therefore, dependent on the advice of those who represent the interest of business to help them understand what is needed from government to promote economic growth and prosperity. Wall Street is one of those special pleaders. The financial industry is critical to all areas of the economy to develop and maintain growth and prosperity in an ever increasing completion for the world's production.

Recently, I watched the drama of congress question Wall Street executives about their business practices and excessive compensation. I could not believe my ears. Questions posed to these executives were made to fit the answers provided to the executives by these executives. The questions were not Main Street questions, like who lost all that earned money that you received as compensation? Why was it that these investors were as stupid as to expose their life's savings to almost total loss? Investors who lost their money to Wall Street were not stupid; they lost their money to stealth transactions by self-dealing insiders. Main Street questions have not been answered by congressional investigators.

The one way that congressional investigators ask such un-informed questions is that they are provided scripted questions written by sympatric advisors. So, how do sympathetic advisors access the ears of Congress? Wall Street insiders don't buy votes! They don't have to buy votes. They are hired as advisors. They are invited to populate the committees that write the legislation. Their specialized knowledge provides legislators the expert infor-mation that makes Congressional legislation useful to Wall Street. Wall Street lobbyists write the script and legislative actors play the scene. This is Hollywood drama and just as phony. As expert advisors to the committees that write the legislation, laws can be enacted that are deliberately flawed, and difficult, if not impos-sible, to reverse or revise within a time frame required to protect the public's interest.

The Santa Rosa Chronicle published an article by Common Cause, Wall Street Lobbying Fed Congressional Apathy. Accord-ing to the article, $180 million in lobbying fees and campaign contributions were made by Fannie Mae and Freddie Mac to help persuade Congress to finance their bailout. The top five mortgage brokers and bankers provided $31 million in campaign contri-butions and lobbying fees in 2008 to help get support for their congressional bailout. You have heard of the Wall Street criminal Bernard Madoff, have you heard of Senator Boughtoff and Rep-resentative Paidoff? What script will congressional leaders follow? The pitiful script of 20,000 families losing their homes to preda-tory lenders or the script presented by bankers with $31 million?

How did these financial predators get away with their sleazy frauds? The same way that Wall Street insiders and corporate managers are cashing out billions of dollars in gift shares from shareholders' money. With the help of their expert advisors, their congressional sponsors wrote the legislative script that legitimized their theft. Congressional leaders in the finance committees were guided by a complete instruction manual of Acts and Omissions for Market Manipulations by Financial Insiders' for financial insiders' market manipulations. Excuse me, they call it financial innovations!

Because Wall Street insiders do not buy votes, does not mean that a financial interest is not exchanged. How does a politician negotiate a cashless exchange of value for value with Wall Street insiders? The process is as old as politics. The children of congressional leaders are favorite candidates for lobbying jobs. Besides the millions of dollars contributed to Vice-President Biden's political campaign, his son has made a fortune as a lobbyist. A company hired Speaker of the House Nancy Pelosi's son with no experience and made him a "Strategic Planner" for over a hundred thousand a year. The revolving door of congress members retiring from Congress to work as lobbyist is a Washington joke.

When Wall Street pays out hundreds of millions of dollars in lobby money and campaign contributions, they seek a quid pro quo. The Lectric Law Library, http://www.lectlaw.com/def2/q003.htm, defines QUID PRO QUO—Lat. 'what for what' or 'something for something.' The concept of getting something of value in return for giving something of value. However, a direct quid pro quo exchange between a politician and a Wall Street firm is forbidden. So, politicians work around the law to a legal indirect exchange of patronage. Patronage is the act of providing sponsorship and protection to favored individuals. The process is institutionalized in the form of quid pro quo patronage (qpqp) where political connections create the illusion that no politician is bought-off or paid-off for their votes.

Three recent cases of quid pro quo patronage make the point. It can be argued that the following three people where the most qualified for their government positions, but from another perspective, it can be argued that they were most qualified to represent the interest of Wall Street.

Bush and Obama's Self-dealing Appointees

Henry Paulson, ex-CEO of Goldman Sachs was politically connected to ex-President George W. Bush. , Besides taking bonuses of over $200 million in gift and optioned stock out of shareholders' money, Mr. Paulson's connection to Bush got him appointed Treasury Secretary of the United States. Not only did Paulson write the Goldman Sachs tax payer bank bailout script for Congress, but the bailout of Goldman Sachs helped to save Goldman's management bonuses. His script provided legitimacy to bailout and covered up the Crimes of Wall Street insiders'. Conflict of interest? Absolutely!

President Obama appointed Larry Summers, his director of his National Economic Council. Summers is the perfect appointment to advise the president, if you own a hedge fund. According to Tyler Durden, http://www.seekingalpha.com, in 2007 Summers traveled to Asia as a pitchman for hedge fund D. E. Shaw recommending to investors the purchase of toxic collateralized debt obligations (CDOs). His sales tour was timed just weeks after the collapse of Bear Sterns hedge fund. The CDOs were collateralized with defaulting subprime loans.

According to Robert Scheer, www.truthdig.com, Summers received $8 million in 2008 paid to him by Wall Street firms through speaking engagements. As treasury secretary for the Clinton administration, Summers opposed regulations that would have prevented the toxic derivatives market crises. He received some 8 million thanks as recognition for his Wall Street work. Would you trust this guy to wash your car? Not if he could find a way to make a buck from your car's parts!

President Obama's appointment to the Securities and Exchange Commission was not much better. Mary Schapiro, was a poor choice for a good reason, while serving a director on the boards of Kraft Foods and Duke Energy, she received thousands of awarded (gift) shares. Certainly, she is aware that the money she cashes out of these gift shares comes from Mom and Pop 401 (k) funds. Would she, as head of the SEC, question the legitimacy of such a transaction? If she did, she would have to indict herself. Schapiro's connection to Wall Street brought about her appointed to the SEC. The adverse consequences for Mom and Pop investors are predictable.

Lobbyist and political appointees are in a position to form and style Wall Street's version of the regulatory environment. The next time Wall Street creates a financial crisis, their lackeys, as appointed expert regulators, will clean-up the mess, and then the scripting process will start all over again. They will be looking for a new direction and new opportunities. The public will be lulled back into their pipe dreams by the Wall Street piper—until the next time. But don't forget! You'll have to pay the piper.

April 28th 2009
Madoff the Thief:
(Pronounced Made-off)
By
Michael R. La Crone

There once was a thief named Madoff,
His honesty he did trade-off:
Before you blame, for all the shame,
Don't forget Bought-off and Paid-off.

Bernard Madoff stole $50 billion from investors in a financial Ponzi scheme and got caught.

He could not steal that much money without the help of many people who had the authority and responsibility to stop him. The questions are, who are they? Where are they? And why haven't they been brought before a court?